A Practical Guide to
Distributed Processing Management

AUERBACH Data Processing Management Library

James Hannan, Editor

•

Contributors To This Volume

Grayce Booth
Honeywell Information Systems Incorporated
Phoenix AZ

James W. Conard
Conard Associates, Costa Mesa AZ

Dr. James C. Emery
Professor, Wharton School, University of Pennsylvania
Philadelphia PA

Kenneth A. Hamilton
Vice President, Manufacturers Hanover Trust Company
New York NY

Samuel B. Harvey
Senior Vice President, Rude, Harvey, Schwartz and Associates
Haddonfield NJ

Joseph Hazen
Assistant Vice President, Manufacturers Hanover Trust Company
New York NY

John R. Kessler
Deere & Company, Moline IL

William E. Perry
CPA, CIA, CISA, President, William E. Perry Enterprises Incorporated
Orlando FL

Joseph Podolsky
Palo Alto CA

Joseph G. Robertson
Director of Advanced Systems, Rockwell International
Corporate Information Systems Center, Seal Beach CA

José A. Trinidad
Telecommunications Specialist, Philadelphia PA

Raymond P. Wenig
President, International Management Services Incorporated
Framingham MA

A Practical Guide to

Distributed Processing Management

Edited by James Hannan

AUERBACH Publishers Inc
Pennsauken NJ

VAN NOSTRAND REINHOLD COMPANY
New York Cincinnati Toronto London Melbourne

Copyright © 1982 by AUERBACH Publishers Inc

Library of Congress Catalog Card Number 82-11623

ISBN 0-442-20900-2

All rights reserved. No part of this work covered by the copyright hereon may be reproduced or used in any form or by any means—graphic, electronic, or mechanical, including photocopying, recording, taping, or information storage and retrieval systems—without written permission of the publisher.

Printed in the United States of America

Published in the United States in 1982
by Van Nostrand Reinhold Company Inc
135 West 50th Street
New York NY 10020 USA

16 15 14 13 12 11 10 9 8 7 6 5 4 3 2

Library of Congress Cataloging in Publication Data
Main entry under title:

A Practical guide to distributed processing management.

   (Auerbach data processing management library ; 8)
   1. Electronic data processing—Distributed processing. 2. Electronic data processing—Management. I. Hannan, James, 1946- II. Series.
QA76.9.D5P73   1982   001.64'404'068   82-11623
ISBN 0-442-20900-2 (pbk.)

Contents

Preface vii

Introduction ix

Chapter 1   A Definitional Framework for Distributed Processing

        Samuel B. Harvey 1

2   Managerial and Economic Issues in Distributed Processing

        Dr. James C. Emery 15

3   Establishing Controls in a Decentralized Environment

        Kenneth A. Hamilton & Joseph Hazen 33

4   Planned Migration to Distributed Systems

        Grayce Booth 49

5   Designing the User System in a Distributed Environment

        Joseph Podolsky 59

6   User Chargeback Procedures for Distributed Systems

        William E. Perry 73

7   Establishing Standards for Distributed Processing

        Grayce Booth 85

8   Designing an Integrated Communications Network

        José A. Trinidad 97

9   Protocols and Compatibility for Distributed Processing

        James W. Conard 111

Contents

10 Information Confidentiality in Distributed Systems
John R. Kessler 123

11 Operational Costs in Distributed Systems
Raymond P. Wenig 137

12 The Relationship between Distributed Processing and Office Automation
Joseph G. Robertson 145

Preface

In its relatively brief existence, the computer has emerged from the back rooms of most organizations to become an integral part of business life. Increasingly sophisticated data processing systems are being used today to solve increasingly complex business problems. As a result, the typical data processing function has become as intricate and specialized as the business enterprise it serves.

Such specialization places a strenuous burden on computer professionals. Not only must they possess specific technical expertise, they must understand how to apply their special knowledge in support of business objectives and goals. A computer professional's effectiveness and career hinge on how ably he or she manages this challenge.

To assist computer professionals in meeting this challenge, AUERBACH Publishers has developed the *AUERBACH Data Processing Management Library*. The series comprises eight volumes, each addressing the management of a specific DP function:

A Practical Guide to Data Processing Management
A Practical Guide to Programming Management
A Practical Guide to Data Communications Management
A Practical Guide to Data Base Management
A Practical Guide to Systems Development Management
A Practical Guide to Data Center Operations Management
A Practical Guide to EDP Auditing
A Practical Guide to Distributed Processing Management

Each volume contains well-tested, practical solutions to the most common and pressing set of problems facing the manager of that function. Supplying the solutions is a prominent group of DP practitioners—people who make their living in the areas they write about. The concise, focused chapters are designed to help the reader directly apply the solutions they contain to his or her environment.

AUERBACH has been serving the information needs of computer professionals for more than 25 years and knows how to help them increase their effectiveness and enhance their careers. The *AUERBACH Data Processing Management Library* is just one of the company's many offerings in this field.

James Hannan
Assistant Vice President
AUERBACH Publishers

Introduction

In the early days of commercial computing, the size, cost, and technical complexity of computer systems dictated the development of centralized data processing facilities in most organizations. Requests for application systems were funneled through these central facilities. DP personnel designed, built, and ran these systems at a pace and in a manner designed to accommodate the central computer's capabilities and limitations.

While computers were a novelty and their applications limited, the DP department was able to satisfy most user information needs with this arrangement. As users became knowledgeable about computers and more aware of their applicability to a variety of business problems, however, the DP department was inundated with demands for more and better systems. The now-entrenched centralized DP structure could not respond as quickly or effectively as users thought it should.

Fortunately, a solution lay just over the technical horizon. Advances in engineering and solid-state technology gave rise to computers that were smaller, faster, more powerful, and less expensive than their mammoth forebears. These so-called minicomputers proved to be both a blessing and a curse for DP managers and users alike. Although the new machines promised to reduce the DP department's applications and processing backlogs, they posed serious problems of standards, compatibility, and control. And for those users who gleefully smuggled minis into their departments in a quest for more responsive systems there lurked an unpleasant surprise—effectively operating the new machines required far more technical expertise than users had.

Enter distributed processing. Theoretically compelling, the concept of distributed processing seeks to weave minis, mainframes, software, communications, and data base technology into a responsive, secure corporate information system. Unhappily, the road to such a DP utopia is strewn with technical, procedural, and managerial obstacles. This volume of the *AUERBACH Data Processing Management Library* is designed to help DP professionals charged with planning and administering a distributed system avoid those obstacles.

We have commissioned an outstanding group of DP practitioners to share the benefits of their diverse experience in distributed processing. Our authors have written on a carefully chosen range of topics and have provided proven, practical advice for managing distributed processing more productively.

In Chapter One, Samuel B. Harvey convincingly refutes what has become almost an article of faith in some DP circles: that distributed processing is so nebulous it cannot be adequately defined. His "A Definitional

Introduction

Framework for Distributed Processing" offers a practical guide that most distributed processing planners will find very useful.

In addition to a useful conceptual framework for distributed processing, planners and administrators need a high level of managerial and technical skill. In Chapter Two, Dr. James C. Emery outlines the economic and managerial considerations that must be taken into account when implementing and administering a distributed system.

Chief among the managerial considerations in a distributed/decentralized environment is the issue of control. While decentralized units must have a degree of autonomy to profit from decentralization, some level of central control is needed to ensure that the activities of individual units do not work against the overall policies and goals of the organization. Based on their experience in a large banking organization, Kenneth A. Hamilton and Joseph Hazen discuss a strategy for establishing controls in a decentralized environment in Chapter Three.

Many organizations approach distributed processing through the expansion and/or evolution of existing centralized applications. While expanding existing systems is ostensibly less risky than implementing a totally new distributed system, the requirements for migrating current programs, data bases, operating methods, and the like into the new environment can be very complex. Management support of migration planning is needed to minimize the risks. Grayce Booth discusses the management and planning considerations for distributed systems migration in Chapter Four.

No matter how they evolve, distributed systems can provide users with improved service and greater control over computer resources. In Chapter Five, Joseph Podolsky examines distributed systems from the user's viewpoint and details the important user-oriented characteristics of distributed processing. In Chapter Six, William E. Perry discusses the design of user chargeback systems that, when properly administered, aid management in allocating, promoting, and restricting the use of computer resources.

Planning for distributed processing must also include specific plans for setting and enforcing standards. Because a distributed network involves multiple computers, it is all too easy to develop incompatible procedures, programs, and documentation. In her "Establishing Standards for Distributed Processing," Grayce Booth sets down the reasons for standards, points out areas for standardization, and describes practical standardization methods.

The nerve center of any distributed system is its communications network. The current immaturity of telecommunications technology makes the process of designing a network more complex and delays the formulation of a coordinated solution to communications problems. In the face of these conditions, organizations designing a network for distributed processing should ensure that their design can grow with the developing technologies

Introduction

of the 1980s and 1990s. In Chapter Eight, José A. Trinidad presents a design methodology that can help planners develop such a network.

An important component of the network planning effort is the area of communications protocols. In his "Protocols and Compatibility for Distributed Processing," James W. Conard addresses the issues of compatibility inherent in integrating network components and facilities of different suppliers and discusses current efforts to alleviate these problems.

Protecting confidential data is an important concern when dealing with distributed systems. Controls encompass both organizational and procedural issues, including consideration of such elements as return on investment, development methodologies, vendor selection, design alternatives, and education. In his "Information Confidentiality in Distributed Systems," John R. Kessler discusses these elements in order to help developers implement the required security measures in distributed systems.

In addition to the direct, visible costs associated with distributed systems (e.g., equipment, space, operators, maintenance), there are also many indirect costs (e.g., media, education, systems support). Many of these costs can be controlled and significantly reduced through proper planning. In Chapter Eleven, Raymond P. Wenig discusses operational costs for distributed systems and the steps that can be taken to control them.

Besides distributed processing, the computer industry has devised another major strategy to increase productivity—office automation. Many organizations with distributed networks will eventually be faced with the task of integrating office information systems into these networks. Joseph G. Robertson outlines the relationship between these two types of information system and includes practical suggestions on how to prepare for their eventual integration.

1 A Definitional Framework for Distributed Processing

by Samuel B. Harvey

INTRODUCTION

Several people in the DP industry believe that distributed data processing (DDP) can be all things to all people. Each vested interest can make its own definition to suit its own purpose. To some, in fact, distributed processing is a buzzword created to sell hardware. This lack of clarity would not matter if DDP were just a fad. DDP is not a fad, however; it is a clearly identifiable trend that will become the principal method supporting all information processing. Definition, therefore, becomes very important. It is impossible to plan for something that is not well defined. The purpose of this chapter is to provide an analytical framework for understanding and classifying distributed systems.

HISTORICAL DEVELOPMENT

The first electronic computer was built in 1946, and by the early 1950s, business and government began to use computers. The original systems estimators felt that a relatively small number of large, powerful machines would perform vast quantities of work because of their high-speed electronic capabilities. It quickly became apparent, however, that even at electronic speeds, computers had definite limitations. The early expectations of large integrated files from which any combination of desired information could be pulled at random were abandoned. The more realistic approach of batching information on relatively slow magnetic tapes was adopted to keep this valuable piece of hardware busy.

Although batch processing suited machine operations quite well, it often inconvenienced the user whose operation, unfortunately, was not batch. Information was sometimes late, often not combined in quite the desired manner, and frequently difficult to access. These problems often resulted in lost business opportunities. Although the value of computers could not be denied, users became increasingly frustrated by the restrictions imposed by the machine.

Users were further restricted by the type of organization that evolved to control the DP function. Equipment value was high, the cost of programming and operating the equipment even higher. Applications were expensive and took a great deal of time to develop. Given these realities, it was necessary to institute tight, organized, *central* control.

While users were wrestling with the computer's idiosyncrasies, a series of new concepts were built or programmed into equipment in the 1950s and 1960s: simultaneity, multiprogramming, multiprocessing, operating systems, communications monitors, and high-level languages, among others. The objective of these developments was to make big electronic CPUs more efficient. Hardware development was so rapid that, by 1965, the DP industry had seen three generations of hardware. Although each generation was technically superior to its predecessor, the rigors of conversion aggravated already strained user relationships.

Rapid technological change also posed major problems for systems professionals. They had to cope with increasing complexity in such areas as communications, data base, operating systems, application specialties, performance monitors, and operations research. The management of these interrelated areas required specialized knowledge and well-developed management skills.

The need for specialization also widened the gap between the systems professional and the user. In the early days of DP, many systems people were drawn from the business ranks to learn DP. With increased complexity and specialization, however, it became necessary to hire people trained specifically in DP. Unfortunately, these specialists had very little business experience. They were faced with the difficult task of keeping current in a complex technical field while understanding the needs of business users.

Enter DDP

Given the historical problems associated with DP, the need for a new support system that could be modularly designed and tailored to the user's information requirements was obvious. Several developments, which proceeded independently, combined to create the base for a new support environment:

- Large data-utility hardware—Large utilities can process many jobs simultaneously. These utilities automatically access multibillion-byte files. The utilities also have communications capabilities that make them economically accessible to many people, regardless of their geographic locations.
- Communications—Technical advances in the movement of information over various communications links (e.g., satellites, optics, microwave) provide the capability to transmit information in such large quantities and at such reasonable costs that various geographic locations become insignificant.
- Minicomputers—The power and price/performance ratio of minicomputers make it economically and operationally feasible to literally design computer systems around small groups of people performing limited, specific functions.

A DEFINITIONAL FRAMEWORK

- Intelligent terminals and microcomputers—Low-cost computational capability has been developed at each terminal, along with the ability to tailor terminals to human needs.
- Software—Currently the weakest link in distributed systems, software is showing very positive trends:
  —Comprehensive communications multicomputer network systems are being developed.
  —Nonprocedural user-oriented languages are being developed.
  —Data base, random-oriented file systems are maturing.

A FRAMEWORK FOR DDP

The developments described in the preceding section suggest an analytical framework within which to understand DDP. Distributed processing can be conceived of (and defined) as a group of subsystems—processing, networks, software, data base, standards, and control—each with its own functions, yet operating in concert to provide users with more flexible and responsive systems for their business and information needs (see Figure 1-1).

Processing (Hardware)

There are two classes of distributed hardware:
- Class I systems are connected to a communications network. Most distributed systems have (or will have) a communications capability and some logical reason to pass information to another part of the company (or to share corporate resources).
- Class II systems are unique to a particular function and are not connected to any ancillary operation. These are independent CPUs that are not part of any master plan.

Distributed Hardware—Class I. There are two types of Class I computer hardware organization: hierarchical systems and distinct-linked systems.

Hierarchical systems are characterized by multiple levels of computational power. For planning purposes, the most common number of levels is four:
- Level 1—Data Utility. The utility can run many programs and may contain several processors (from one or more vendors). The computer complex can access multibillion-byte files and has a front-end communications capability. The underlying purpose of the utility is to provide modular growth. The utility should provide remote services for transaction processing, time sharing, and RJE if and when required. A typical Level 1 configuration is shown in Figure 1-2.
- Level 2—Satellite System. The system can perform four simultaneous functions:
  —Multiple RJEs to a Level 1 (if and when required) by way of high-speed lines (9,600 baud)
  —Local batch processing (if and when required)
  —Servicing multiple online real-time terminals interactively and pass-

CONTROL	SOFTWARE	PROCESSING	STANDARDS	COMMUNICATIONS NETWORK	DATA BASE
Equipment Selection Planning DBMS Operations System Use Application Development Audit Security & Privacy Financial Authorization and Approval Cost Distribution and Benefit Centralized/ Decentralized Project	Central/Local Implementation & Maintenance Scheduled Predetermined Output Query on Demand Decision-Support Output (local)	Independent System (single system) Hierarchical- (interconnected) Different Levels (large, medium, small terminals) Multiple Related Systems	Security Privacy Backup & Recovery Design & Development Methods DB Management Type of Equipment Operating Systems Communications Programming Documentation Procedures Training	Star Tree Point to Point Combination Ring-Mini to Mini	Central Replicated Partitioned Combination

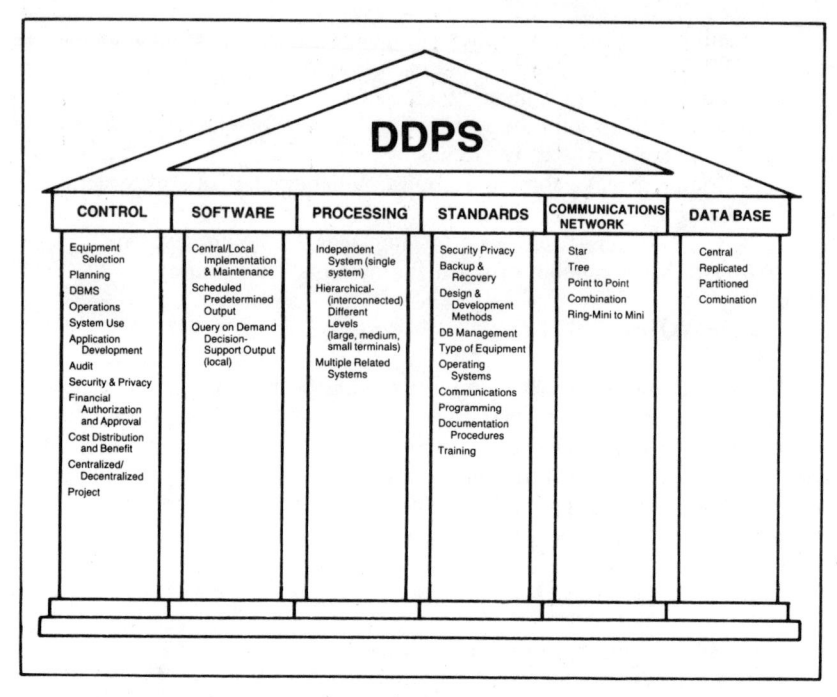

Figure 1-1. The Six Elements of Distributed Data Processing Systems

ing messages to other processors

—Performing all message switching necessary to accomplish the preceding tasks

By definition, Level 2 systems range from $30,000 to $300,000 in price. A typical Level 2 configuration is shown in Figure 1-3.

- Level 3—Intelligent Terminal. There are two types of intelligent terminals: specialized and generalized.
  —Specialized terminals contain minicomputers built to handle a specific application (e.g., point of sale [POS], factory data collection, teller terminals, reservation terminals). The terminals are programmable and can handle a variety of peripheral devices.
  —Generalized terminals are small, powerful miniprocessors capable of performing all of the functions of a Level 2 system, except at a reduced capacity. Level 3 processors can approach 500K bytes of high-speed memory and can support a full range of potential peripherals. System costs are generally less than $30,000.
- Level 4—User Terminal. For our purposes, a user terminal is the means by which the human interacts with the electronic system. User terminals can be keyboards, printers, video displays, TV sets, media readers, sensors, voice response units, or even push-button pads. Most future terminals will contain powerful microprocessors that are easily adaptable to people. The price of a Level 4 will range from $10 to $3,000. A typical Level 3 and Level 4 are shown in Figure 1-4.

A DEFINITIONAL FRAMEWORK

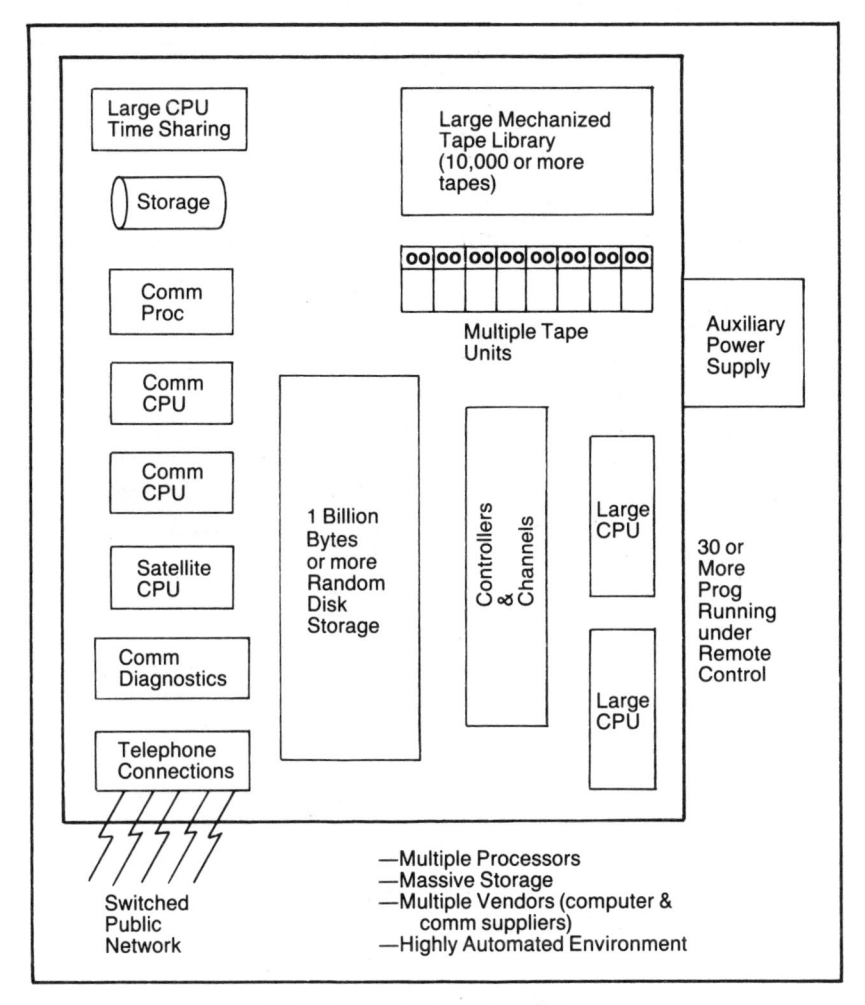

Figure 1-2. Typical Level 1 Site

Diagram contents:
- Large CPU Time Sharing
- Storage
- Comm Proc
- Comm CPU
- Comm CPU
- Satellite CPU
- Comm Diagnostics
- Telephone Connections
- Switched Public Network
- Large Mechanized Tape Library (10,000 or more tapes)
- Multiple Tape Units
- 1 Billion Bytes or more Random Disk Storage
- Controllers & Channels
- Large CPU
- Large CPU
- Auxiliary Power Supply
- 30 or More Prog Running under Remote Control

—Multiple Processors
—Massive Storage
—Multiple Vendors (computer & comm suppliers)
—Highly Automated Environment

The hardware architecture for Levels 2 and 3 is generally engineered to support interactive terminals and a high degree of multiprogramming. Some processors have hardware operating system features.

Most hierarchical systems maintain a degree of central hardware control at the host. A common network control point is sound theory, provided reasonable flexibility within the system is maintained.

In distinct-linked systems, each system operates within a distinct environment. Occasions to pass information between systems may arise, but, generally, applications are self-contained. An example is a hospital with communicating, but independent, machines in the various medical departments. A system of processing for distributors, each independent but linked to a common source, is another example.

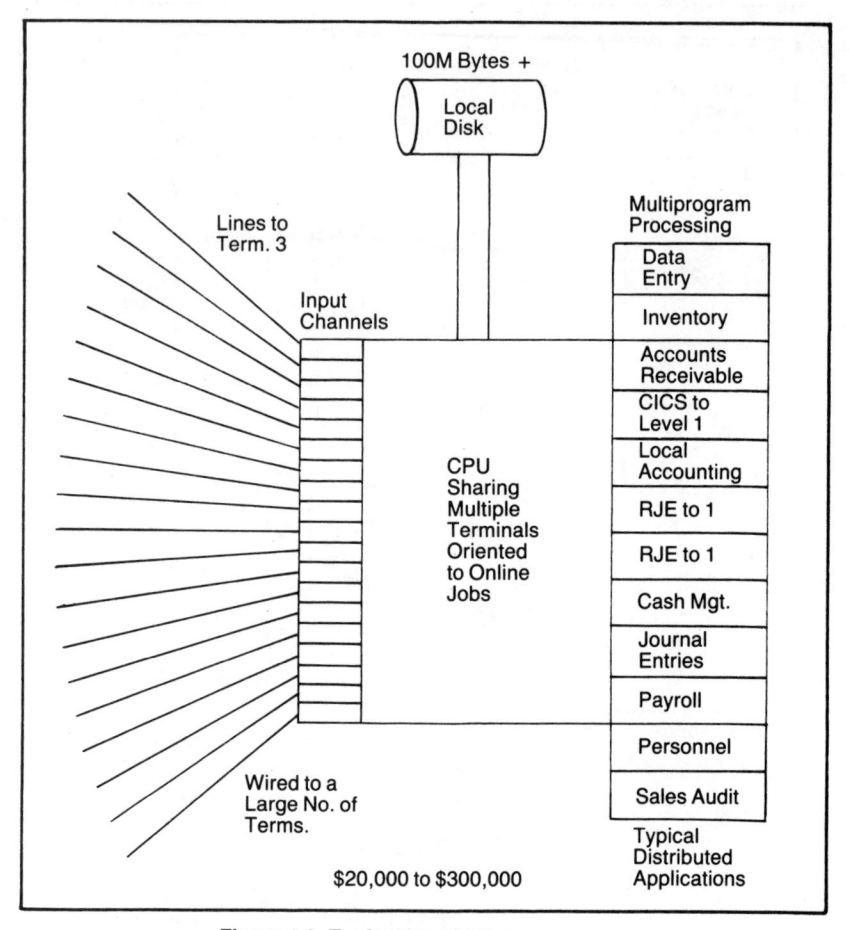

Figure 1-3. Typical Level 2 Processor

Distributed Systems—Class II. There are systems that process independent applications that have no relationship to any other processing—there is no reason to communicate. The nature of the specialized function may dictate a completely independent approach to solve a problem. Some scientific applications are in this category, as is process control equipment.

Networks

If computers are the bricks of distributed systems, then communications networks are the mortar. Communications make distributing the processing a reality. The magnitude of change in communications and the corresponding increase in communications capability are even greater than are advances in the computer hardware field.

Because the communications environment is so complex, further classification is required to define, analyze, and organize the functions. For our

A DEFINITIONAL FRAMEWORK

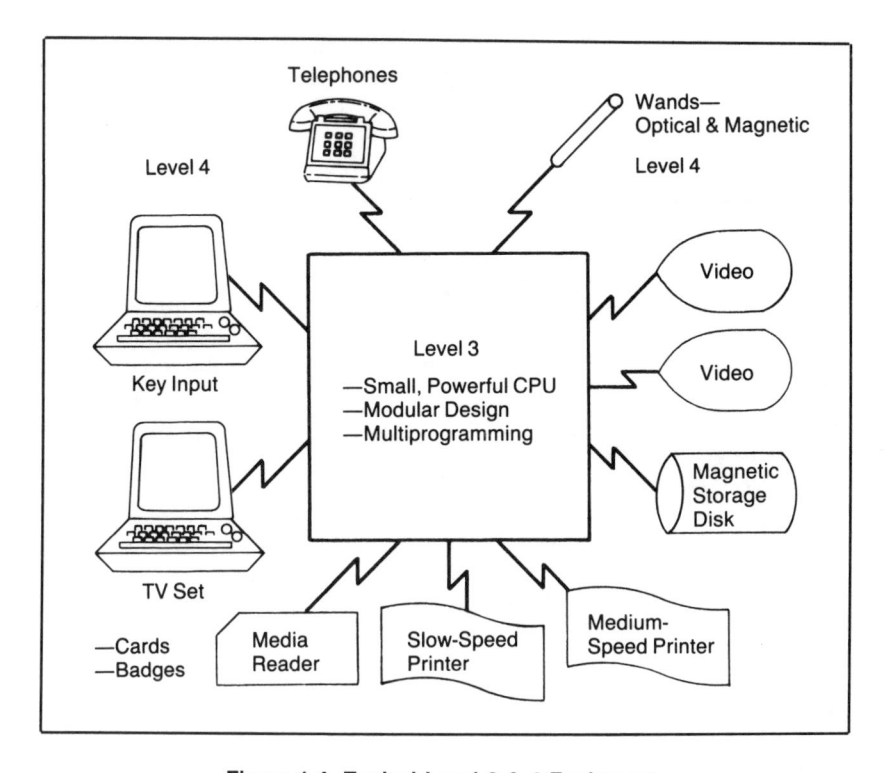

Figure 1-4. Typical Level 3 & 4 Equipment

purposes, this classification scheme is appropriate:
- Classes or spheres of communications (areas being serviced)
- Communications architecture (how systems are designed)
- Communications elements (the composition of communications)

Classes or Spheres of Communications. Communications can be segregated into three analytical spheres. Each sphere has distinct characteristics, although they can be bound into a total system:
- Premise loops—These are the communications within buildings; this sphere of communications is not regulated. Technological advances, mainly in the areas of coaxial cables and fiber optics, are important for this area. The integration of a number of currently independent premise-loop systems into single networks is likely to occur in the near future. The current internal telephone system, office of the future, DP terminals, and video conferencing are key areas that will be affected.
- Local loops—These are communications within cities and specific geographic areas (i.e., the local links between houses, office buildings, hospitals, schools, and factories). The phone companies are the principal suppliers, although CATV companies are an expanding service; microwave suppliers represent a new potential.

- Long distance—These are the channels that link remote areas. Traditionally, they were primarily telephone long lines for voice and, later, high-speed data; slow-speed data was Teletype or TWX. Recently, microwave and satellites have made communication of large quantities of information feasible and economical.

Figure 1-5 illustrates a system composed of the three spheres.

Distributed Communications Architecture. A communications architecture is composed of fundamental design elements, which, in turn, are combined in a blueprint for a total structure. The architecture should be designed to handle current requirements and to allow for expansion. Examples of design elements are:
- Network structures
  - Point to point
  - Ring
  - Star
  - Tree
  - Combinations
- Network organization techniques
  - Store and forward
  - Packet switching
  - Circuit switching
  - Multiplexing
  - Compression
  - Encryption
  - Data under voice
  - Digital voice

Examples of total architectures are:
- Manufacturers' designs
  - IBM's System Network Architecture (SNA)
  - Digital Equipment Corporation's DECNET
  - Sperry Univac's Distributed Communications Architecture (DCA)
  - AT&T's Advanced Communication System (ACS)
- User designs—These can be service operations, individual users, or consortiums of users, including:
  - ARPANET
  - Telenet
  - Tymnet
  - Cybernet

From the maze of available alternatives, each user must select the options that fit the specific organization. The resulting design may be a combination of architectures.

Selecting and designing an architecture is a long-term decision. Because architectural changes are difficult and very expensive, design objectives should be projected for at least 20 years. Changing elements within an architecture is not difficult if the original planning was careful. Without such a

A DEFINITIONAL FRAMEWORK

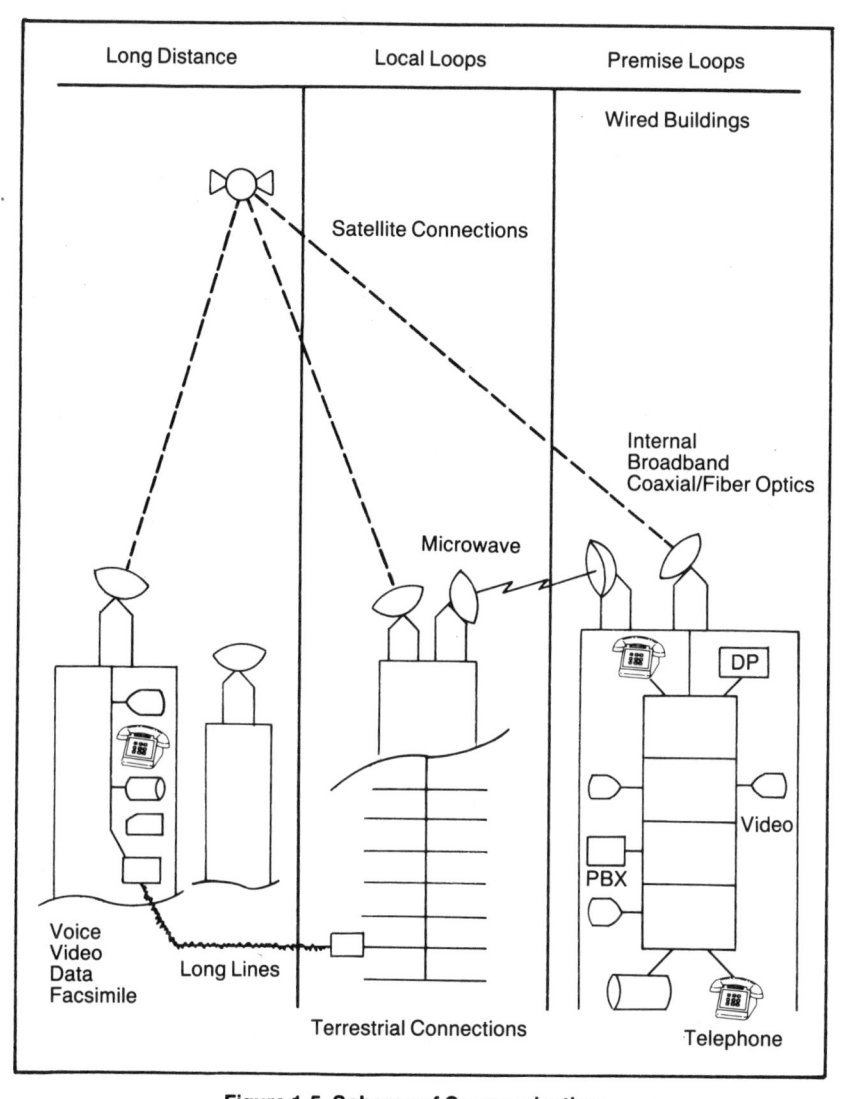

Figure 1-5. Spheres of Communications

long-range design, coordinating systems in multiple computers will be costly and cumbersome and will afford the user few options.

Communications Elements. These are the physical elements—electronic boxes and transmission channels—that enable communications. Included among the electronic boxes are switches, controllers, modems, CPUs, satellites, earth stations, and terminals. Transmission channels include fiber optics, coaxial cables, twisted pairs, satellite frequencies, and microwave. Between the processing boxes and channels there must be memory to store information as it passes through the system.

The elements of a communications system are constantly changing because of rapid technological development. As stated earlier, the objective of the systems planner is to allow insertion of new developments into an architecture that changes much more slowly. Achieving this objective is possible through careful, thorough planning.

Software (Systems and Applications)

Systems software coordinates, drives, and controls the computer/communications network. Systems software includes such items as operating systems, teleprocessing monitors, communications systems, language processors, and service routines.

During the past 25 years, systems software has become so complex that its cost has consumed a major percentage of the savings realized from decreased hardware costs. The large, complicated, centrally oriented systems were designed primarily to increase the efficiency of expensive central CPUs. Distributed systems create a completely new environment. The systems problem is more complex because of the number and diversity of elements that must be controlled. The problems, however, are better understood, and the problem-solving tools have much greater power and flexibility.

The trend in distributed processing is toward putting systems software into firmware and also into distributed processors. Using an independent processor to perform a given function avoids the contention problems introduced by multiprogramming, enabling more predictable operating results. In addition, with modular design, a small additional processor can be introduced to increase power, providing an alternative to replacing a large system to achieve the same results.

Because the operating systems in distributed processing will proliferate through multiple CPUs and terminals, compatibility among the equipment of competitive vendors becomes a problem. A series of studies designed to address the problems of compatibility are a high-priority item.

While distributed systems raise important issues about systems software, the key questions about distributed systems address applications software:
- How do distributed systems affect users?
- Is there a difference between a distributed and a central system in terms of business operations?
- Is the information support to the business operations stronger?
- Are distributed systems a mere technical phenomenon, or do they represent new business opportunities?

At this juncture in the evolution of distributed systems, it is safe to assert that they do represent new opportunities. POS networks are a good example of the new opportunities provided by distributed systems. POS systems, which now service nearly one million retail customers, became practical when the computer was put in the cash register in 1968 and was then tied into communications networks. Thus, some order and intelligence were supplied to the application.

More general advantages in the applications area are also apparent:
- Line production operations can now have online terminal support and are less vulnerable to CPU failure.
- Input can be validated at its source, eliminating errors that would otherwise be propagated through the system.
- Central control can be effectively implemented by downloading central applications to remote processors and monitoring activity from a central site. Most large retail POS systems are organized in this fashion.
- Conversely, it is possible to allow users to develop their own applications so that applications will not adversely affect each other and can be clearly charged to the originator.

Parallel developments in applications programming promise to extend the advantages of distributed systems to users. For the most part, programming has been a highly technical activity requiring a good working knowledge of the equipment on which the programs run. The programmer usually translates user specifications into code that can be executed on a computer. Trends in software, coupled with new hardware capabilities, are changing this traditional approach.

A new level of programming—nonprocedural languages—is emerging in which the programmer will no longer have to tell the machine how to fulfill user needs; this step will be automated. In this new environment, the programmer will have to be more familiar with users' needs and ways of doing business than with particular equipment. A new type of programmer-user relationship will emerge. The manner in which this new relationship develops in a distributed environment must be carefully planned and monitored if users are to realize the benefits of more direct interaction with their systems.

Data Bases

The concept of the integrated file, touted in the 1950s as the primary goal of DP, has been resurrected under the rubric data base. The underlying tenets of both concepts are the same: information should be managed as a corporate resource, data should be independent of programs, and storage redundancy should be reduced. Until recently, these goals were unrealizable because the equipment could not handle the load that the goals imposed.

Distributed processing can help solve the problems of equipment limitations. Through combinations of specialized modular file processors, distributed computers handling terminals, and distributed communications networks with modular design features, the hardware bottleneck can be opened.

The data base approach is still in the early stages of development; continued research and experience are necessary to fully understand how various data bases will be organized and coordinated on a distributed basis.

Standards

The need for standards in all fields is obvious, but nowhere is it more crucial than in DDP. Unfortunately, several powerful forces in the DP industry are working to discourage and, in some cases, subvert standardization efforts (i.e., engineering innovation, the competitive desire for product differentiation, rapid technological change, and intense market competition). The problem is real because DDP and networks cannot function without standards.

Communications Standards. Communications standards are essential for DDP. Transmitting information among various computers over several types of carriers requires precise interfaces and protocols. Sadly, the current situation is not encouraging. Hardware interface standards are difficult to promulgate because so many vendors desire uniqueness, both for marketing and engineering reasons.

Each vendor also has its own protocols. Either a standard must be developed that defines message formats (the electronic pulse patterns that identify the message, the error recovery procedure, and the message handling systems), or a method must be designed that permits the attachment of nonstandard devices to a given system.

Perhaps the most difficult area in the field of communications standards is communications software. The software architecture of distributed systems is not within a single computer but extends into multiple CPUs and even into intelligent terminals. Designing such an architecture is a complex task for a single vendor supplying multiple processing levels; it is many times more complex with various competitive equipment. Advances in this area must await further research and development.

Software Standards. It has been difficult to develop effective application software standards because users seem always to be clamoring for program changes to meet their specialized needs. Many DP/MIS managers feel that this problem will be compounded in a distributed environment, as remote users write their own programs with little or no regard for standards.

Standardization is also difficult in systems programming. The different sizes, uses, and configurations of equipment make it difficult to have standard operating systems. As a result, the processing environment between and among systems is often very different. The ideal solution may never be realized. The goal of minimizing intercomputer complexities that do not contribute to a system's utility to the user will be a continuing quest.

Data Base Standards. Data bases that are independent of operating programs containing the basic information of the enterprise will be part of all future systems. Standards are required to help preserve the integrity and control the use of the information. Once again, the issue is complicated by the variety of distributed equipment. The organization and handling of data bases is a major specialty in itself that requires continuing analysis.

Language Standards. More work has been done in language standardization than in any other area. Such standardized languages as COBOL,

FORTRAN, BASIC, and Pascal have been extended to distributed equipment. The development of nonprocedural languages that enable users to communicate directly with the information system will require the same level of standardized effort—the end user has neither the training nor the inclination to deal with nonstandard conditions.

Hardware Standards. For much of its history, the computer industry has witnessed a curious cycle: large, expensive machines have periodically (about every six years) been developed to replace the then-current large, expensive machines. Since it has always been impractical to rewrite the equipment's massive software systems, the new hardware was designed to run the old software. The old software, unfortunately, did not utilize the full capabilities of the new equipment.

Users encountered another problem when their equipment ran out of capacity. The only solution was to replace their systems with even larger ones. The incremental steps between generations of hardware were often very large and left many users bewildered.

Distributed processing and networks have significantly altered this historical pattern. Entire networks cannot be replaced periodically. Imagine the chaos attendant upon replacing a large POS or hospital system every six years or so. In this environment, growth comes from modular addition rather than from replacement; this requires a new set of standards.

Architectural Standards. Because we are still in the early stages of designing and building distributed information networks, the architectural standards for building them have yet to be developed. Until an orderly framework is established, much effort will be expended in uncoordinated efforts that will likely fall short of achieving the real advantages of DDP.

Control

Perhaps no other aspect of DDP raises as many questions or concerns as does control. Essential issues tend to become lost in the swirl of anxieties created by most debates about control. To understand the issues involved, we must ask ourselves two sets of questions: one set from an information manager's viewpoint, the other from the point of view of a line manager. Control questions that an information manager must ask include:
- Must all of the equipment be in one room in order to be controlled? (Doesn't the phone company exert central control over distributed equipment?)
- Who should control data bases?
- How should we treat such issues as standards, downloading, auditing, remote diagnostics, polling, centralized communications, system network architectures, and monitoring?
- Who should be responsible for applications programming today and in the future?

A line manager must ask such questions as:
- Do distributed manual operations enable tighter operational control than that of distributed computerized operations?
- Are manual standards easier to enforce than automated ones?
- Are companies going to change their basic organizational philosophies because of a computer system?
- Did control of the business only evolve with the advent of a centralized computer system?

The answer to some of these questions may surprise many managers. For one, the control philosophy of most businesses was established long before that business acquired computers. Organizational control has not changed materially because of computers, nor is there any indication that businesses are reorganizing around computers. In addition, control of a geographically dispersed computer/communications network is not the Byzantine enterprise it is often portrayed as—it is a straightforward, manageable process. Furthermore, when information managers really analyze control of input from distributed manual operations and from distributed automated operations, they will soon realize that it is easier to control input from distributed computers.

CONCLUSION

In order to understand such a complex concept as DDP, it is useful to divide it into categories. For DDP, these categories are discrete subsystems, operating together to form an integral distributed system. We have identified six such subsystems and have outlined the broad dimensions and crucial issues of each. To understand the present and the future of distributed systems, one must carefully track developments in these subsystems. This "modular" approach to understanding the concept will prove a valuable aid in designing, implementing, and managing an actual DDP system.

2 Managerial and Economic Issues in Distributed Processing

by Dr. James C. Emery

INTRODUCTION

The fantastic rate of development in computer and communications technology opens vast new opportunities for implementing more cost-effective information systems. With opportunities come pitfalls, however: an advance in technology can be applied badly. This is especially true of distributed processing. The distribution of processing power and data throughout an organization can provide more responsive and cost-effective computer support for users; it can also add many new problems of coordination and implementation as well as cause a growth in grass-roots applications of dubious value. The proper use of technology in a distributed environment calls for increased knowledge and wisdom on the part of managers and technicians alike.

ALTERNATIVE PROCESSING CONFIGURATIONS

Technological developments over the past few years have enabled various new alternatives for system designers. The older approaches—primarily decentralized standalone computers or shared centralized computers—may still be attractive under certain circumstances, but now designers should also consider hybrid configurations that combine some of the characteristics of both centralized and decentralized systems.

Centralized Systems. In its extreme form, a centralized system locates all processing within a single computer and all system development work within a single organizational unit. The data base is similarly concentrated (although usually it is physically split among a hierarchy of storage devices and logically fragmented among application areas). Remote users may be served by the physical transport of input data (e.g., handwritten input forms) and output reports; increasingly, however, users are linked to the central system by electronic means, constituting a so-called "star network." (Remote users need not be geographically distant from the central computer; organizational separation, rather than geographical distance, is the essential characteristic of the remote user.) In a completely centralized system, the central staff provides all technical services and also plays the dominant role in setting development priorities and allocating existing computing resources among competing demands.

Decentralized Systems. Opposite the completely centralized system is the completely decentralized system in which no communications links exist among multiple standalone computers. Each organizational unit having a computer supports the system with its own funds and is totally responsible for development and operation.

Variations of Centralized/Decentralized Systems. Systems rarely exist in a purely centralized or decentralized form; they usually have some elements of both. Four basic combinations are possible, as indicated in Figure 2-1.

Even within these basic combinations, considerable variation is possible. For example, decentralized system development and operation may be constrained by centrally imposed standards dealing with such matters as procedures for cost/benefit justification, equipment selection, design and development methods, documentation, programming languages, and operating procedures. Similarly, management of a centralized computer center may be influenced by such factors as a policy committee composed of users or a budgeting scheme that permits users some control over their computing expenditures (or even over the choice between the central computer or an external supplier). Furthermore, the degree of centralization need not be uniform throughout the organization; for example, a major component of a company (e.g., the consumer products group) may be decentralized with respect to

		Program Development	
		Decentralized	Centralized
Computer Operation	Decentralized	Pure decentralization	Centralized development of application packages for execution on standalone equipment at the user's site
	Centralized	Centralized information utility that provides raw computing services to decentralized application programmers	Pure centralization

Figure 2-1. Basic Combinations of Centralization and Decentralization

corporate management but highly centralized with respect to its own subdivisions (e.g., the electrical appliances department, refrigerator department).

Distributed Systems. Although the term is often used to describe anything from a centralized star network to a completely decentralized system, it is useful to limit the definition to systems with the following characteristics:
- Multiple processors with general-purpose computing capabilities (possibly with a supporting local data base).
- Communications links (often only intermittent) among the processors.
- Relatively weak interactions among the distributed subsystems, which typically serve separate organizational subunits. (This characteristic excludes tightly coupled processors working in parallel on a cooperative computing task. Although many of the technical issues involved in designing a tightly coupled system are analogous to those of a distributed system, the organizational problems may be quite different.)
- Considerable centralized coordination in the design and operation of separate processing subsystems.

Variations in Distributed System Design

A variety of systems fall within the set of characteristics just listed. The principal alternative configurations are indicated in the following sections.

Distributed Processing without Local Data Bases. The most basic form of a distributed processing system is one in which some local processing occurs without the support of a local data base. Any auxiliary storage (e.g., cassette or floppy disk) is limited to storing various routines, input formats, and edited transactions. A typical example is a distributed data entry processor. The local processor prompts the data entry clerk by displaying the data elements required for a given transaction type. The data entered is usually subjected to various editing checks that do not require access to the central data base (e.g., range and mode checks); in particular, a master record to be updated by an incoming transaction is not accessed during first-level editing. Edited transactions are usually stored temporarily in a transaction file and transmitted periodically, perhaps daily, to the central computer for further processing (generally requiring access to the central data base). If it is worthwhile to reduce the input lag, transactions can be transmitted in frequent batches or even individually (perhaps based on a priority code that governs the transmission delay).

Hierarchical System with Nonshared Local Data Bases. In addition to providing local computing, a distributed processor may also maintain a local data base. This is an especially attractive design (because of its simplicity) if the local data base contains data not required elsewhere in the system and is updated from local transactions. An example of such a system is a local plant-wide processor that stores a detailed data base pertaining to such matters as plant inventories and production schedules, hours worked by plant employees during the current pay period, and transaction-level accounting data. The distributed processor may handle all local processing, usually including some online applications (e.g., data entry) and one-time inquiries requiring access to the local data base (e.g., an inquiry on the inventory status of a given raw material). Summary data is periodically transmitted to a central site that handles system-wide processing and maintains a central data base. For instance, the central computer might generate weekly aggregate production schedules that take into account overall production requirements and the existing status of each plant. A schedule could then be transmitted to each individual plant, where it is broken down into a more detailed schedule based on the detailed data stored in the local data base.

Rather than being updated from local transactions, a local data base may be updated by replacing it periodically with a more current version of an extracted subset of the central data base. This might be a useful approach, for example, in a bibliographic retrieval system in which new entries are added each day and retrieval concentrated in several geographically separated locations. Such a design may be justified on the basis of reduced communications and processing costs (compared with online access to a distant central processor).

Distributed Segmented Data Base with Limited Remote Access. In some cases, a transaction that originates at one location may require access to data maintained at another location. This design is attractive if there is a relatively low probability of having to access the remote data base; if this is not the case, a central data base is likely to be more efficient. In a bank system, for example, each branch may keep the current account balance of only its own local customers. If a customer wishes to cash a check at a branch other than his own, the transaction must be transmitted to his own branch to determine whether the account has sufficient funds to cover the check.

To initiate a transaction, a local processor must be able to identify the remote processor that maintains the data base to be accessed. This problem is greatly simplified if the transaction itself contains identifying information (e.g., an account number that uniquely associates a customer with his local bank). Unfortunately, using an external identification number to locate data often builds in unacceptable rigidity, so a more flexible means must often be used. The alternatives are a sequential search (until the desired item is found) of the directory of local data maintained at each site, the creation of a central directory that gives the location of each record, or the maintenance at each site of a duplicate copy of a global directory. The optimum design in a given situation depends on such factors as the frequency of directory updates and inquiries, the cost of communications, and the cost of central versus local storage. Sharing even a relatively simple distributed data base can raise difficult problems (e.g., synchronization among data bases, the avoidance of deadlocks, and file security and privacy).

Multiple-Level Hierarchical Distributed System. Any local processor in a distributed system can itself be a central node of lower-level distributed subsystems. For example, a microprocessor in a petroleum refinery that controls a distillation operation might be linked to a plant-wide minicomputer that controls intraplant material flows; the plant computer, in turn, may be linked to a corporate-wide center that handles interplant scheduling.

Fully Distributed Network. The alternatives discussed so far are based on a logically centralized design in which certain functions are physically distributed; they have a hierarchical structure, with a single computer playing a central role. A fully distributed network has no central focus but rather is composed of multiple autonomous processors that have equal control status (although they may vary widely in their computing capabilities). Their purpose is to allow resource sharing by separate processors.

The network provides a market in which various services can be bought and sold, with the cost of the services providing the primary means of allocating resources and regulating supply and demand. Hardware economies may motivate some of the network traffic (e.g., load leveling or economy of scale in performing very large "number crunching" jobs). A much more likely application, however, is the opportunity to share specialized programs and data bases. Examples of resources that might be shared include econometric models and data bases, specialized engineering design programs, computer-assisted instructional materials, and bibliographic data bases. A distributed network also provides a mechanism for person-to-person communication among remote sites by means of an electronic mail system.

Other Possible Distributed Configurations. Every information system consists of a collection of functional tasks. In principle, the tasks can be arbitrarily distributed among multiple processors and data bases. In practice, however, problems of coordination, synchronization, reliability, and security may become overwhelming unless the distributed components are largely independent of one another. If a task interacts strongly with other tasks (through coupling or shared resources), it is usually better to handle that task within a single processor and data base. Thus, if one subsystem supplies another with high-volume data inputs having very short response-time requirements, the two activities should usually be processed within a single computer. Similarly, if such functions as marketing, engineering, manufacturing, and accounting share a common data base with multiple logical links among data elements, it is extremely unlikely that maintaining duplicate copies of the data base among functionally oriented distributed processors would prove attractive (or even technically feasible at the present time).

CENTRALIZATION VERSUS DECENTRALIZATION

A distributed system is best viewed as a cross between centralization and decentralization. With suitable design, it can provide many of the advantages of both centralized and decentralized systems—and can avoid many of their disadvantages. It is useful, therefore, to present the arguments in favor of each approach.

Arguments (and Counter-Arguments) for Centralization

Hardware Economies of Scale. The traditional argument that computer hardware provides substantial economies of scale is no longer very persuasive in most cases. Because hardware constitutes a declining share of total cost, potential economies of scale in hardware have a declining effect on systems design. The availability of very cost-effective minicomputers alters the traditional relationship between capacity and cost and further reduces the pressure for ever-larger computers (although the huge computer-bound tasks found in some branches of science and engineering will no doubt always provide an incentive for expanding the capacity of the largest computers). Auxiliary storage stands as an important exception to the declining significance of hardware economies: very large storage devices continue to provide economies of scale and an incentive to centralize large data bases.

Operating Economies of Scale. Certain operating costs exhibit substantial economies of scale. For example, the personnel costs of computer operators, clerical staff, systems programmers, maintenance engineers, and management rise less than proportionally with increases in the size of the computer, provided the variety of functions performed remains relatively constant. Thus, a single computer center would almost surely be significantly less expensive to operate than would two or more regional centers that provide a similar full range of services. Frequently, however, growth in center size is accompanied by an increase in the number and variety of the services it offers. This can add enormously to the complexity of the system and the costs of operating and maintaining it—and can substantially reduce possible operating economies of scale.

More Powerful Capabilities. A central computer center can support a wide range of services that would be prohibitively expensive to provide at each of several smaller centers. Programmers and designers have become accustomed to powerful operating systems, communications software, data base management systems, application packages, generalized utilities, and programmer aids. Stripped-down minicomputers cannot offer such services. Their less-powerful range of services may reduce programmer productivity or call for a downgrading in the functional specifications of application programs. If minicomputer applications are simple enough, the lack of sophisticated programmer support services may not be too serious; temptations often arise, however, to add to complexity. To overcome some of their limitations, minicomputer facilities have a habit of growing in size and complexity—and can easily reach an annual budget of several hundred thousand dollars.

Less Total Capacity. The peak load at a centralized computer center is usually less than the sum of the peaks if the same load were distributed among several facilities (unless all peaks coincide, which is unlikely). Thus, the capacity required to provide a given level of service at a central computer is apt to be less than the aggregate capacity needed if demand is split among two or more separate centers. Similar arguments for centralization apply in the

MANAGERIAL AND ECONOMIC ISSUES 21

case of a real-time system that must process randomly arriving transactions within a given response time.

Reduced Number of Facilities. Some difficult management problems arise when the total computing load is fragmented. Hardware maintenance, backup capacity, and physical security become much more serious problems when processing is geographically dispersed. By concentrating all of its efforts at a single centralized site, management can more easily provide around-the-clock maintenance, backup capacity, and tight physical security.

Development of Professional Staff. Highly competent systems professionals usually prefer to work with colleagues having similar interests. A central group can more easily achieve a "critical mass" of professionals who work together productively and provide a rich cross-fertilization of ideas. A large central staff can support specialists, who can then be assigned on a temporary basis to given projects. The fragmentation of technicians among decentralized subunits makes it much more difficult to attract and retain competent technical personnel. Assignment to a decentralized subunit may be ideal for someone primarily interested in the career ladder within the subunit; for a person committed to a technical career path, however, a remote assignment may make it more difficult to keep current with technical developments and to compete for advancement with technical personnel who remain in the central staff.

Increased Systems Integration. One of the most persuasive arguments for centralization is that it allows a higher degree of integration than would otherwise be possible. For one thing, centralization fosters the integration of DP by means of increased data and hardware sharing, reduction of undesirable redundancy in a common data base, and consolidation of processing functions (e.g., payroll and personnel). Centralization also facilitates the coordination of organizational activities by providing an organization-wide data base and a more powerful processor capable of handling sophisticated planning and control systems.

Arguments (and Counter-Arguments) for Decentralization

Although a strong case for centralization can often be made, the unfortunate fact is that most centralized systems fail to live up to their potential. Large central computer centers are too often inhospitable and unresponsive. They tend to grow continually in size, complexity, and organizational distance from the ultimate user. In reaction to these problems, users often favor a more decentralized system, even at the expense of some lost potential savings from the centralized approach. Although by no means a panacea, decentralization does offer some important advantages.

Greater Control by Users. The most appealing argument for decentralization is that it moves control of the system nearer to the ultimate users. A decentralized manager can allocate resources and set priorities more in line with the goals of his subunit, rather than conform to the goals of a central group. Contention with other subunits is eliminated so that urgent needs can be satisfied (within the limits of capacity) without coordinating and bargaining with external parties. The system can adapt to changing needs without negotiating with external groups affected by the change. The argument that equivalent or better service can be provided at lower cost by a central computer carries little weight with a lower-level manager who has previously experienced poor service from a central facility. Unfortunately, the expected increase in control and responsiveness of a decentralized computer may often prove illusive, since the small computer often has limited capacity and provides less powerful means to implement effective systems.

Increased Motivation and Involvement of Users. The perception of greater user control, along with the greater simplicity usually offered by a decentralized system, often results in increased user involvement in the operation of a decentralized facility. Users are much more inclined to participate in design decisions and may sometimes even program their applications. The widespread availability of interactive terminals and user-oriented programming languages fosters such participation and provides an incentive for users to acquire the skills needed to take advantage of current technology. Furthermore, a well-designed decentralized system is likely to become an integral part of daily operations; users thus have a strong motivation to make it work successfully by such means as providing high-quality input data and participating in the correction of design imperfections.

Involvement of this sort is an essential ingredient of a successful system, but, if not adequately controlled, it may have an unfavorable side as well. For example, user control may result in unnecessary duplication of existing applications, waste of programming time, inefficient and ineffective systems because of lack of professional qualifications among decentralized personnel, and hidden costs of systems development.

Economies of Specialization. The argument for decentralization is greatly strengthened if fragmentation permits simplification of each part of a system. Simplification reduces the cost of hardware, systems software, application program development, and operations. A minicomputer dedicated to interactive BASIC applications, for example, can often get by with a fairly modest amount of primary and auxiliary storage. Only a small staff is required to operate the computer and maintain its relatively simple system and application programs; it may even run unattended through parts of the day and operate with virtually no software maintenance, beyond infrequent updates to a turnkey system. Similarly, a computer system specialized for chemistry calculations, for example, can avoid unneeded hardware (e.g., high-speed I/O facilities), languages (e.g., COBOL), user services (e.g., program consultants), and other overhead costs associated with a large full-service computing center. A specialized online application on a dedicated minicomputer can often be developed at less than one-quarter of the cost that would be required to append it to a finely tuned centralized system. Finally, a specialized system can substantially reduce the problems of coordination across organizational boundaries and charges for shared resources.

Exploitation of Low-Cost Micro- and Minicomputers. The cost advantage of micro- and minicomputers stems from their relative simplicity, their large-volume production (enabling production economies of scale), the limited services furnished by their vendors, their ability to incorporate recent technology (because of their relatively short design and production cycle), and the keen competition in the marketplace. As a result, these computers offer an extremely attractive price/performance ratio for a variety of jobs. The cost advantage enjoyed by micro- and minicomputers largely depends, however, on their being applied to relatively simple tasks. This, in turn, often comes from the segmentation and specialization achieved through decentralization.

Small Increments to Capacity. Because of the limited capacity and low cost of minicomputers, they can usually be added to (or enhanced) in small steps and at low incremental cost. Their delivery lead times from vendors are generally considerably shorter than those of large computers. Capacity adjustments can therefore be made fairly quickly in response to existing or anticipated changes in demand. This fact may substantially reduce the "safety factor" that must be added to expected demand to avoid unacceptable congestion. Additions to capacity can incorporate state-of-the-art technology, thus allowing a relatively close tracking of technological advances. In contrast, large computers are typically installed infrequently and in relatively large-capacity increments. This tends to increase excess capacity and lengthen the average age of the technology used.

Reduced Communications Costs. A self-contained decentralized computer center has little need to communicate with other parts of the organization. Consequently, communications costs are low, compared with those of a centralized system linked to remote terminals.

Reduced Interactive Response Time. A centralized system serving a variety of users on a time-sharing plan tends to give relatively unpredictable response times. The load on the machine may vary widely throughout the day, seriously affecting service. Both the mean and the variance of response time may be increased because of possible lags in the communications links between the central processor and its remote terminals. A decentralized system, however, reduces or eliminates some of the sources of time lag. Allocation of capacity is under closer control of users, so the load can often be limited in order to meet response time requirements. In the extreme case of the personal computer dedicated to a single user—which is becoming less extreme as the costs of electronics continue to drop—competition for resources among multiple users ceases to be a factor in response time variability.

Increased Reliability. Decentralized systems tend to be less complex than centralized systems, and with simplicity comes reliability. A decentralized system does not depend on communications lines, which are often one of the least reliable components of a central system serving remote terminals. Increased component reliability, the modest cost of redundancy (e.g., spare circuit boards), and ease of maintenance (e.g., user-diagnosed board replacement) further add to the attractiveness of small decentralized systems. Then, too, the fact that a failure in one part of a decentralized system does not cause failure throughout the organization reduces the penalty when downtime occurs. These advantages are offset, at least in part, by the high cost of providing professional maintenance support at each of several decentralized sites; in comparison, the cost of such support at a large central facility tends to be relatively low. Superreliable systems, which may require complete duplication of all critical components and a complex operating system to handle switch-over and recovery procedures, are also usually less expensive to operate on a centralized basis.

Increased Predictability of Costs. The costs charged to a decentralized subunit for services obtained from a central computer are often subject to considerable variation. Costs may be influenced by such factors as level of use, priority level, time of day, the aggregate load on the machine, the efficiency of the center, and changes in the hardware configuration. Managers of a decentralized subunit often feel that they lack close control over many of these sources of variation in cost. In contrast, a decentralized system dedicated to a single organizational subunit tends to have quite predictable costs. The hardware is often purchased or acquired on a long-term lease, making capital costs entirely predictable. Technical and operating personnel may be under the complete budgetary control of the subunit, so there are few surprises with respect to salary costs. Supplies and other variable cost components tend to be relatively small or subject to management control. Thus, the total cost of a decentralized computer center tends to be predictable and controllable (although the allocation of costs among individual users may vary). This simplifies budgeting for computing and eases management concern about the risks of installing computer-based systems. Budgeting and pricing techniques can be employed by a central computer center to provide a similar predictability in costs—such as a long-term contract at a fixed annual charge for a given fraction of a machine's capacity—but these techniques are not widely used.

Limited Potential Savings from Centralizing Independent Organizational Activities. Centralizing the mainstream activities of an organization can yield benefits if its subunits achieve more efficient resource sharing and more tightly coordinated activities. If, however, only weak interactions exist among the subunits—that is, if they neither supply each other with input nor find it advantageous to use common resources—the potential benefits from centralization are relatively meager. Since centralization always involves some cost, it should not be adopted unless significant savings can be achieved. Under these circumstances, decentralization is especially appropriate because it would not result in reduced integration of organizational activities.

ADVANTAGES OF DISTRIBUTED SYSTEMS

The great appeal of a distributed system is that it offers many of the advantages and avoids some of the disadvantages of the centralized and decentralized approaches. Being a hybrid, a distributed system can centralize some functions and decentralize others in the best overall combination. In some cases, the system may end up with a relatively high degree of centralization, while in others, decentralization may predominate.

Consider the case of a chemical company that produces various products at multiple plants. Most daily interactions within the firm are likely to occur at the plant level; accordingly, it makes good sense to develop a relatively decentralized plant information system at each location. Aggregate scheduling and coordination of interplant shipments could be handled by a centralized computer on the basis of summary data fed to it from the distributed plant processors. The central computer could also provide large-scale services that could not be economically maintained at the plant level. For example, a centralized data base that is accessible through a powerful data base management system could be provided to support applications that require interrelated data from multiple functional areas. Common engineering programs might also be maintained on a central basis.

Unlike a completely decentralized system, a distributed system of this sort must be designed from a global perspective. A central staff must play a lead role in establishing the overall plan for implementation, imposing standards for communication between the distributed processors and the central computer, participating in the development of common software packages, and maintaining sufficient control of the distributed operations to avoid undesirable duplication and uncontrolled growth.

In summary, a distributed system potentially can provide the following advantages:
- Economies of scale and powerful facilities for applications requiring a large full-service machine, since such applications can be handled on the central machine with the inputs and outputs transmitted over the connecting communications lines
- Increased efficiency of the central facility because of the transfer to distributed processors of tasks for which the large machine is not well suited (e.g., online editing, interactive inquiry)
- Work load leveling by shifting work between distributed processors and the central facility (although in most cases it is less expensive to maintain excess capacity among local processors, which often experience most of the effects of varying loads)
- Incorporation of both user-related experience and technical expertise through the joint development of applications by users and the central technical staff

- Integration of information processing (e.g., consolidation of programs and sharing of common data) on the central facility for applications for which this is more cost-effective than handling the processing on local processors
- Integration of organizational activities through the exchange of (summary) data among hierarchical levels of the system
- Greater user control and involvement in the distributed functions tied closely to their operations
- Economies of specialization within the segmented components that comprise the system
- Simplification and economy achieved by breaking the system into relatively small minicomputer subsystems
- Reduced communications costs because of reduced volume of traffic (because some processing can be handled locally without communicating with the central machine) and increased efficiency (e.g., through intermittent high-speed transmission of stored transactions, postponement of transmissions to off-peak periods, sophisticated data compression)
- Reduced response time for interactive functions performed locally
- Ability to provide required reliability and security through a suitable allocation of tasks among local and central processors
- Increased predictability and control of costs through the use of dedicated local processors for local functions and sophisticated pricing of central services
- Capability to share common software and data bases among distributed processors
- Ability to provide online central support services to distributed computer centers (e.g., "hot line" consulting or maintenance assistance, down-line program loading, computer-assisted user support)

HAZARDS OF DISTRIBUTED SYSTEMS

A distributed system clearly offers many potential advantages, and its underlying technological and organizational concepts are fundamentally sound. Nonetheless, a number of pitfalls lie in the path of any organization bent on developing a distributed system. Management should be fully aware of these hazards.

Creeping Escalation of Capabilities and Applications. Once a distributed processor has been installed to handle a specialized function, there is a natural tendency to add additional applications (often advocated, ironically enough, on the grounds of economy of scale and low incremental cost). What might begin as a limited and cost-effective application may become a miniature general-purpose computer that suffers from many of the complexities and overhead costs of a large central machine without, however, enjoying its attendant economies of scale.

Hidden Costs. As a distributed system evolves, users may assume a growing role in its design and operation. As desirable as this is, it also can result in a substantial expenditure of bootlegged time that is not explicitly identified as a development cost. Management thus does not have an opportunity to judge whether the development cost is justified on the basis of expected benefits.

Undesirable Duplication and Incompatibility. If each group having a distributed processor is permitted to proceed on its own without suitable control, unnecessary duplication occurs. Independently developed systems usually cannot share common software and data, provide backup for one another, or pool common repair parts and maintenance personnel.

Incompetent System Design and Implementation Personnel. If a distributed computer is small, it is difficult to attract and support an experienced and competent technical staff. As a result, if applications are developed locally without access to external technical skills and project management experience, the implementors are unlikely to follow sound and well-known technical approaches or to follow good implementation practices. Each group may commit many of the same errors that the profession as a whole made during its earlier period of development.

Suboptimization. An application that is attractive from the standpoint of a decentralized organizational unit may, in fact, be harmful to the interests of the organization as a whole. Suppose, for example, that a centralized computer center charges full average cost for its services, including the cost of supporting a large program library, sophisticated I/O hardware, and extensive user services. A decentralized group may find it cheaper to install a stripped-down distributed processor than to pay full cost for a portion of the large machine and its extensive support services. The incremental cost of providing equivalent raw computing power on the central machine may, however, be lower than the cost of supporting a separate distributed processor. In this case, total costs would be increased by installing the separate processor, even though the decentralized subunit appears to be saving money. Users of the central machine would end up paying more than they would were the separate processor not installed.

Stretching the State of the Art. One of the principal motivations for installing a distributed system is its relative simplicity. This advantage is lost if distributed functions interact strongly with one another. For example, a closely linked data base cannot be duplicated and distributed among geographically dispersed processors without raising some exceedingly complex, if not insuperable, technical problems. Technical personnel have a history of sometimes paying insufficient attention to technical risk, so the danger exists that an organization might seek to implement an overly ambitious distributed design. There is little justification for excessive sophistication because most benefits of a distributed system can usually be achieved by concentrating on relatively simple and straightforward applications.

GUIDELINES FOR DEVELOPING DISTRIBUTED SYSTEMS

With suitable organization and management, the hazards of a distributed system can be kept within acceptable limits. Generalizations about distributed systems are not very useful because each case depends so heavily on circumstances and the rapidly changing state of the art. Nonetheless, the general guidelines listed in the following sections apply across a wide range of situations and, therefore, should be considered by any organization starting to design a distributed system.

Developing a Master Plan

A master plan should play an important role in the development of any system; it is especially vital in a distributed system, which, by its very nature, must be broken down into relatively independent parts and implemented by relatively decentralized groups. The master plan establishes the structure of the system (i.e., the hierarchy of components that comprise the system and the [grossly defined] interfaces among them). Once this is done, implementation of the components can proceed without detailed daily coordination among separate groups but with confidence that the parts will fit and that unnecessary duplication will be avoided.

A system can be structured along a number of dimensions, including the following:
- Geographical
- Common processing functions (e.g., data entry, communications, or data base management)
- Application-dependent functions (e.g., inventory control or cost accounting)
- Functional organizational responsibility (e.g., marketing or engineering)
- Product-oriented organizational responsibility
- Response time (e.g., interactive or batch)

More than one dimension may be used; for instance, product groups can be further broken down by geographical area.

The significant advantages of distributed processing are achieved when the system is structured in such a way that the distributed components are relatively simple. A structure that merely breaks the total system into smaller-scale versions of a full-service centralized computer (e.g., multiple regional computer centers serving various users) is unlikely to prove cost-effective.

Simplicity in a distributed component can be achieved in several ways. Simplicity is gained by limiting each distributed component to a relatively narrow set of functions that fall within the organizational responsibilities of a single subunit. (The desirability of specialization need not discourage all forms of integration. For example, a dedicated system for online student registration in a college should certainly include such related functions as tuition billing and the preparation of class lists. Similarly, an online order entry system should probably include such functions as inventory control, order picking, and billing.) All programs should be kept as straightforward as possible and should adhere to the principles of structured design. It is especially important to avoid all temptation to resort to "clever" tricks and arcane logic.

Simplicity is also gained by choosing a system structure that results in a high degree of independence between a distributed component and the rest of the system. Such independence is achieved when relatively few low-volume interface variables link the component with the rest of the system. Limited sharing of common data similarly increases independence. Response time requirements for communication among modules is also important: the longer the response time permitted, the greater the independence.

Choosing Components to Be Distributed

The design of any system involves complex trade-offs aimed at finding the best overall balance between cost and benefits. A fundamental trade-off in the design of a distributed system is the choice of functions to be assigned to local processors. Different designs can significantly affect the cost of hardware, systems software, application programs, communications, and operating personnel. Nonmonetary criteria used in judging alternative designs should include response time and quality of service, technical and managerial risks, security, reliability, adaptability to changes in the environment or perceived needs, and political and behavioral effects.

There are no simple shortcuts in making design trade-offs; they require a rather detailed study to estimate the costs and other consequences of each alternative considered. In general, however, the trade-offs favor allocating functions to distributed processors under the following circumstances:

- A minicomputer can handle the function in a relatively straightforward manner (e.g., without resorting to clever techniques to squeeze a complex program into a small processor).
- Fast response time is required—as in real-time applications or applications calling for interactive computer support of a manual operation (e.g., online data entry or inquiry).
- A distributed processor can be maintained at an acceptable cost and level of reliability.
- The volume of transactions handled by the distributed processor is sufficient to achieve a reasonable level of use. (A respected analyst suggests that 10 percent utilization is generally sufficient to justify the installation of a distributed processor.)

An important factor influencing the distribution of functions is the relative difficulty of converting from an existing system. If a function is not currently automated (e.g., if an online data entry system is to replace a manual keypunching system), conversion problems are minimal. This situation often arises because technological advances in minicomputers often make it feasible to implement applications that previously could not be justified. Even if a function is currently included in a centralized system, it may exist as a separable module that can be transferred to a distributed processor with relative ease. If a function is thoroughly intertwined with other parts of the system—which is too often the case, despite the recent emphasis on modular design—conversion to a distributed processor would require a major effort. This might be warranted if the conversion is part of the overall redesign and enhancement of a system, but it should not be done without a full consideration of the difficulty.

Maintaining Adequate Control over System Development

Some central direction is necessary if the parts of a distributed system are to have any hope of meshing together. In certain hierarchical planning and control systems, a high degree of centralization is needed; in a fully distributed system, however, a relatively low level of centralization is desirable, with the primary attention of the central coordinating function placed on standardized communications interfaces and the means of allocating resources through a price mechanism.

The central staff should concern itself with the following matters:
- Provision of central computing services
- Development of integrated applications run on central facilities
- Development and management of the organization-wide data base (managed, typically, by a data base administrator)
- Development of common application packages run on distributed processors
- Development and management of the communications network
- Provision of specialized technical services to assist in the development of distributed applications
- Training in systems-related matters (including the training of managers and technical personnel from decentralized subunits); such training may include in-house programs and seminars, external courses, and degree programs at universities
- Administration of a career development program for technical personnel (including those on permanent or temporary assignments with decentralized subunits); such a program may include maintenance of personnel records pertaining to past assignments and education, scheduling of future training, and assignment of personnel among various centralized and decentralized projects to broaden their experience
- Review of computing budgets
- Approval of major extensions to existing applications (to avoid creeping escalation)
- Hardware selection or approval
- Hardware maintenance
- Documentation standards
- Communications protocol standards
- Security standards

The provison of centralized computing services remains an important component in a distributed system. The central facility is especially suitable for

MANAGERIAL AND ECONOMIC ISSUES

dealing with the following types of applications:
- Very large programs—generally batch processed—for which economies of scale and the availability of powerful hardware and software features are of substantial importance
- Specialized programs or data bases that can more economically be maintained on a centralized basis
- Standard services for organizational subunits with insufficient computing requirements to justify maintaining a distributed processor of their own

A central facility providing services of this sort assumes many of the characteristics of an internal information utility. It typically maintains a fairly broad range of services in response to needs throughout the organization. It often employs a sophisticated pricing scheme that includes such features as differential prices based on priority level and time of day, long-term contracts that stabilize costs for users and revenue for the computer center, output-related prices (e.g., a charge for payroll processing based on the number of paychecks produced rather than on the actual use of input resources), a fixed monthly charge for the "free" use of limited computing services (e.g., small interactive programs written in BASIC), and a complete unbundling of user support services to provide low-cost raw computing capacity. Rationing available capacity on such a facility is usually done primarily through a market mechanism rather than through a nonprice allocation, although some nonprice restrictions are often used as well (e.g., a limit on the size of programs that can be run during the prime shift).

A central service need not be provided through an in-house facility. If total demand for central services falls below the amount needed to exploit available economies of scale, three approaches can be followed:
1. Functions that might better be handled on a distributed processor can be consolidated on a central machine in order to build its load.
2. Central functions can be moved to one or more smaller processors that are not well suited to perform them.
3. An external service bureau can be used for the relatively small portion of the load that benefits especially from the capabilities of a large general-purpose facility.

Each approach may be valid under certain circumstances, but the third approach should probably be used more often than it is.

The central staff should aim primarily at facilitating the delivery of effective and efficient computing services throughout the organization, regardless of the computing source. A service-minded central staff thus should not view itself as an operator of a production facility but rather as a coordinator of computing activities; the physical and organizational location of the hardware should become entirely secondary issues. The conversion from a production to a service mentality is not always easy and often calls for a set of user-oriented skills that are new to many computer center personnel. The transition to this coordinating and consulting role is, however, a key ingredient in a successful distributed system.

CONCLUSION

There is little doubt that distributed computing will be the primary systems architecture of the future. Systems are evolving toward a greater diffusion of processing power and data bases. The advantages of decentralized computing can be further enhanced by linking the distributed parts through electronic communications. Successful implementation of such a system calls for users to develop increased maturity about information technology and for systems management to develop greater management skill and sensitivity to user needs.

3 Establishing Controls in a Decentralized Environment

by Kenneth A. Hamilton
and Joseph Hazen

INTRODUCTION

In the early 1960s Manufacturers Hanover Trust (MHT) developed a centralized, functionally oriented computer operation. In the 1970s MHT reassessed its DP strategy to better serve the needs of particular market segments. Decentralized DP units called vertically integrated data centers (VIDCs) were created. This organization is illustrated in Figure 3-1. In VIDCs, DP activity is *decentralized* rather than distributed. Responsibility and authority for computer operations, technical support, and systems development are at the VIDC level. As this strategy proved successful, MHT continued to integrate the functions of the DP manager and the bank operations process manager, resulting in the formation of vertically integrated operations centers (VIOCs) in 1980. Decentralization made the DP function more responsive to user and customer needs.

The decentralized environment presents new challenges for DP management. Effective policies and procedures must be developed to ensure proper management control and to protect the long-term interests of the organization, while providing each unit autonomy to meet the needs of their specific market segments.

Using Richard Nolan's stage theory of DP development [1, 2] as a model, the following evolution can be expected in a decentralized environment. At first, when central authority is divided among multiple autonomous subunits, all subunits will be similar in structure, practices, and procedures. In time, however, differences will evolve in response to unique business conditions; this divergence may be contrary to the overall objectives of the organization. The purpose of decentralized DP management is to be more responsive to the needs of particular users and/or customers. Achieving this goal may lead to suboptimization of other goals (e.g., cost reduction through economies of scale) and may require sacrifice of "horizontal" efficiency for the sake of "vertical" effectiveness.

Differences will appear in how two subunits achieve similar objectives, and each subunit will probably evolve at a different rate. Management may find it difficult to control such a situation without retarding the most advanced

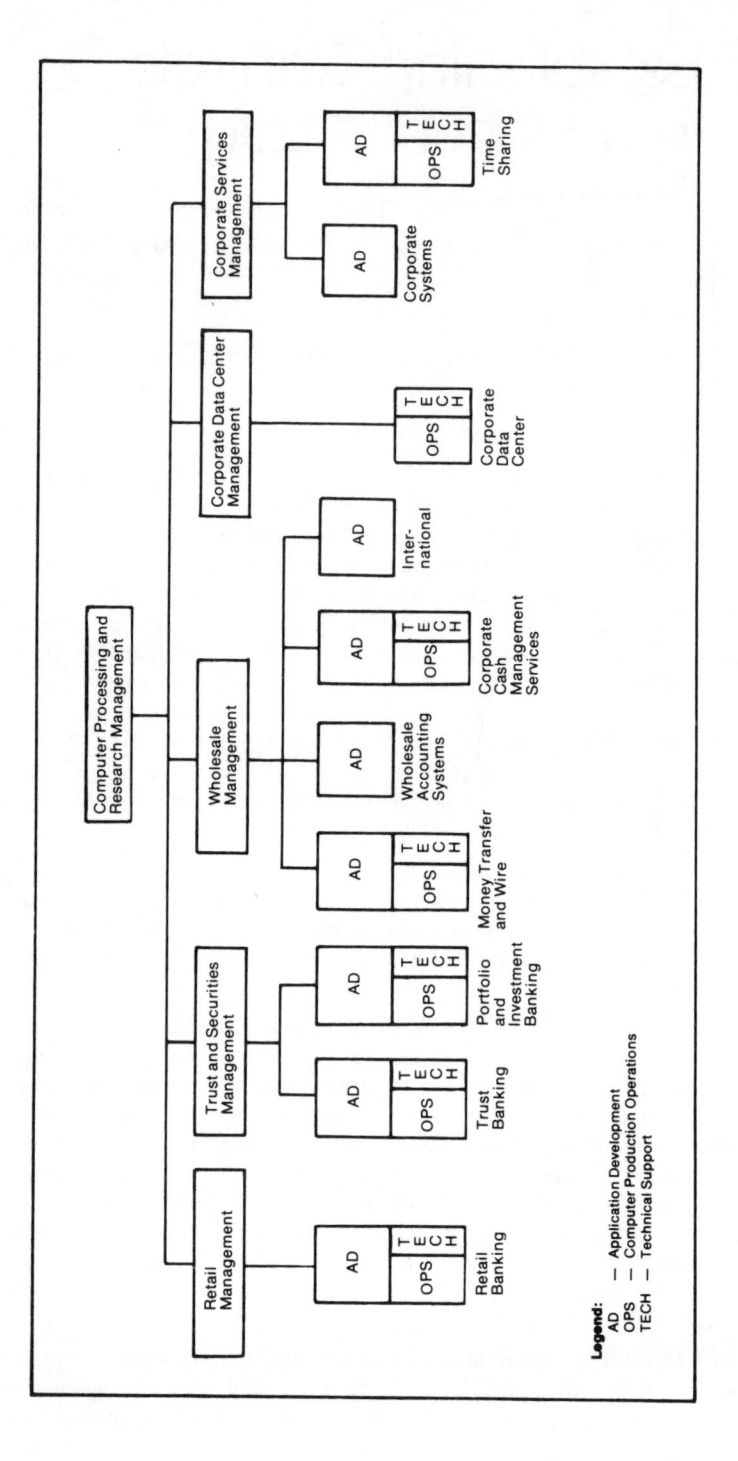

Figure 3-1. VIDC Organization

units. This can have serious consequences—it can increase costs and reduce the ability to respond to competitive pressures in a timely manner.

This chapter discusses the policies and procedures that must be developed, installed, enforced, and maintained to cope with these problems and to ensure the success of a decentralized environment.

DETERMINING THE POLICIES AND PROCEDURES REQUIRED

As the DP organization decentralizes and grows, central control must be maintained at a more highly summarized level. The executive in charge cannot be concerned with the details of items such as project expenditures, staffing, hardware, and software. Responsibility for these must be delegated to the managers of the decentralized units.

From senior management's perspective, broad control must be exercised over cost, risk, and business opportunity. A corporate-level policy statement is needed. Standards developed when the organization was a single centralized unit may now be inadequate.

It is not easy to decide which policies, standards, and procedures (or portions of them) should be retained centrally and which should be decentralized. The decision is partly a matter of management style; however, the most important factor in the delegation of responsibility for policies and procedures may be the maturity of the decentralized units. When a manager first assumes responsibility for a unit, he or she has a host of new concerns and needs the guidance of central policies and procedures. With experience, the manager can evaluate how well these fit the needs of the unit, and at this time, the central authority may delegate responsibility for specific policies and procedures.

It is critical to maintain the overall stability of the organization throughout this process. The decentralized units may go through a series of fairly rapid changes. During this period, it is advantageous to maintain control. Once the rate of change slows, senior management can consider decentralizing control.

Budget and Business Planning

Initially, the budget is the primary means of control. Each decentralized unit and each department within the unit submit an annual budget. Once the budget is approved, adherence is measured monthly through variance reporting. Specific accounts are scrutinized, and any account that exceeds the budget by a given percentage is reviewed in detail.

The business plan documents the work to be delivered for the budget dollars allocated. The business plan for each department is developed in conjunction with the users and defines what development and maintenance work will be undertaken. Ideally, the planning cycle begins with a statement of corporate strategy, and users develop their plans based on that strategy. DP plans, in turn, are developed to support user plans.

Only efforts that qualify as "major deliverables" (i.e., those with an estimated cost exceeding $250,000) or that are key events in the user's business strategy are reported separately on the business plan. Other work is summarized. For each major deliverable, estimated cost and manpower are shown by quarter.

Associated with the business plan is a staffing plan showing total department staffing. This plan is used as input for the human resources function and as the basis for the department's budget.

Although the business plan is developed annually for the same time frame as is the budget, it is subject to formal revision each quarter. Currently, a five-quarter planning horizon, which is updated and extended each quarter, is used. One of the greatest benefits of this arrangement is that the business plans are well established by the time the next annual budget is drawn up.

Steering Committees

Overall control and coordination of DP efforts is monitored by a hierarchical set of steering committees. In the centralized environment, a single DP steering committee performed this function. DP projects were planned in conjunction with informal groups of user management. These relationships have now been formalized in a hierarchy of DP steering committees.

The lower-level (local) committees now have final authority over systems efforts within specified funding parameters. Each decentralized DP unit has one of these committees to oversee resource allocation and establish priorities to meet business needs. Its responsibilities include review and approval of annual budgets, business plans, and projects.

At a higher level is the bank-wide DP steering committee. This committee includes the chairmen of the local committees and other senior bank officers, including the auditor, controller, and corporate planner. Budget, plan, and project approval (at higher dollar levels, involving major deliverables) are this committee's responsibility.

Technical Management Committee. Between these two steering committees is a technical management committee consisting of senior DP representatives from each VIDC. This group is responsible for reviewing the technical aspects of strategies and significant projects to identify technical risks and to ensure that policy is followed. For example, projects that use new technology, require distributed processing capabilities, or involve interaction between data centers are reviewed. If the technical management committee does not approve of the technical direction of a project, the chairman informs the bank-wide steering committee when the project is presented for funding approval. The final decision on the project is made by the bank-wide steering committee.

For projects in which funding requirements are large (i.e., more than $500,000), approval is also required from the bank's senior priorities committee, which is chaired by the chief executive officer.

ESTABLISHING CONTROLS

Division of Responsibility for Policies and Procedures

In general, central policies should govern *what* is to be done; *how* it is done should be decided by the decentralized units. There are, however, compelling reasons to retain some control functions at the central level (e.g., cost-effectiveness, scarcity of specialized resources, or consistency from a senior management viewpoint).

Contract Administration. At MHT contract administration is performed by a central unit. The expertise required to evaluate and negotiate leases and to review contracts is so specialized that it would be impractical to develop it in each unit.

Computer Asset Control. Hardware and software asset control can also be carried out more efficiently at the central level. It is important to DP senior management to be able to establish the organization's DP asset position. In a smaller, centralized environment, this may not be too difficult; in a large, decentralized environment with five major data centers and hundreds of terminals in use, a centralized, automated system is needed.

Project Manpower and Cost Reporting. Collecting information and reporting on project manpower and cost is also a central function at MHT. Since this information is sent to all levels of management from project manager up, it might be considered a logical candidate for decentralization; however, Senior management's need for summarized data in consistent format necessitates a common system.

Project Life Cycle

The division of responsibility for establishing policies and procedures is usually more complex than that described in the preceding sections; often, responsibility is split between central and decentralized groups. The following paragraphs discuss this division of responsibility as it applies to the project life cycle at MHT.

High-level controls over the system development process are maintained centrally, while the responsibility for defining the process and adhering to it rests with the decentralized units, and procedures may differ from one unit to the next.

Some central constraints are placed on the decentralized units. Features such as the names of phases, the outlines for certain phase documents, and certain sections to be covered may be centrally dictated. The dotted line in Figure 3-2 represents the division between life cycle requirements dictated by central authority and those under control of the individual VIDCs. The level of the dotted line represents the degree of conformity to a central project life cycle standard.

The degree of detail used in each phase of the VIDC-specific project life cycles varies from one unit to another. The life cycle in a given VIDC could be represented by Figure 3-3. The height of the rectangle associated with each of the four phases (feasibility, functional specification, design specification, implementation) represents the degree of detail required by that VIDC's standard. Note that a minimum level is required by central policy. In practice, the degree to which the centrally dictated constraints affect different phases of the project life cycle usually varies, as shown in Figure 3-4.

If different VIDCs can have different requirements for the life cycle phases, then each VIDC must be represented separately. Figure 3-5 shows each VIDC with a life cycle that differs in level of detail but that conforms to the central standard.

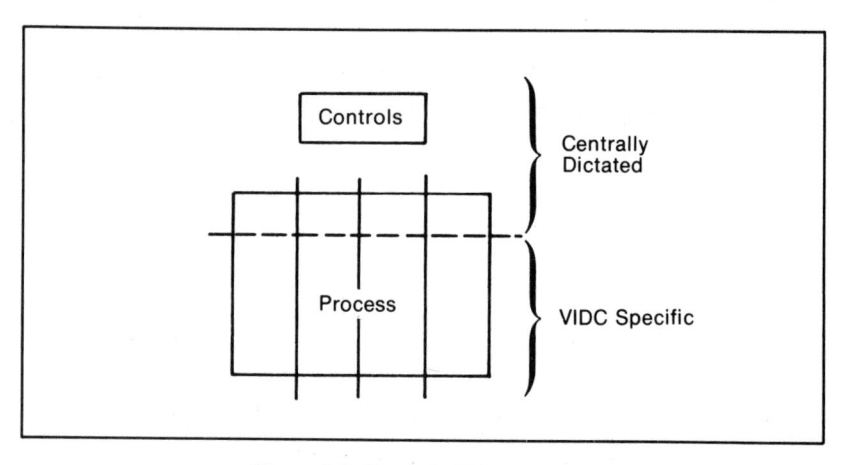

Figure 3-2. Control of Project Life Cycle

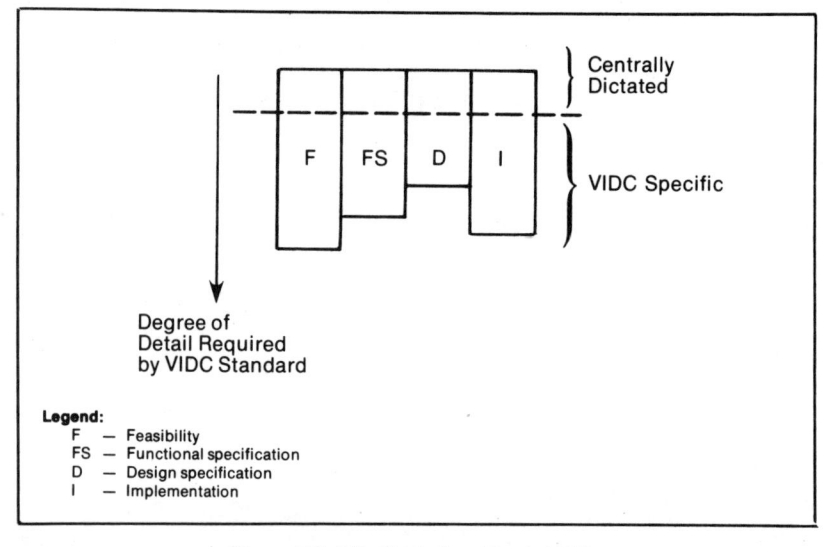

Figure 3-3. Life Cycle in a Single VIDC

Legend:
- F — Feasibility
- FS — Functional specification
- D — Design specification
- I — Implementation

ESTABLISHING CONTROLS

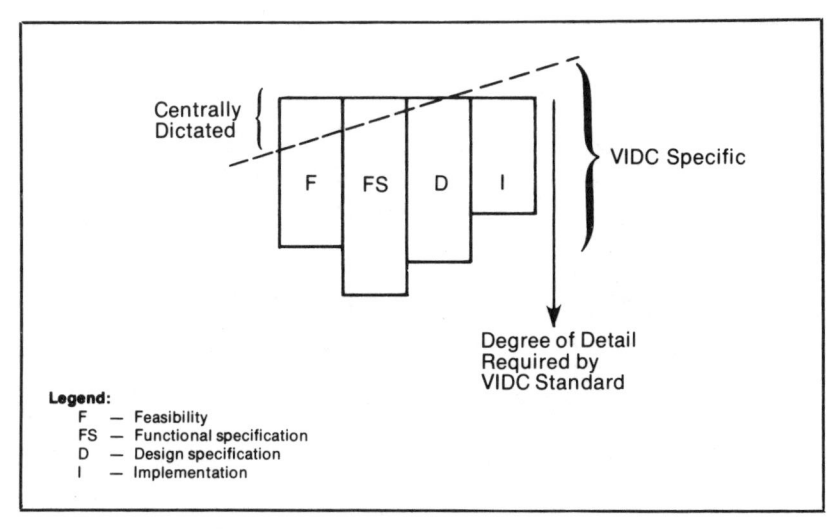

Figure 3-4. Actual Life Cycle for a Single VIDC

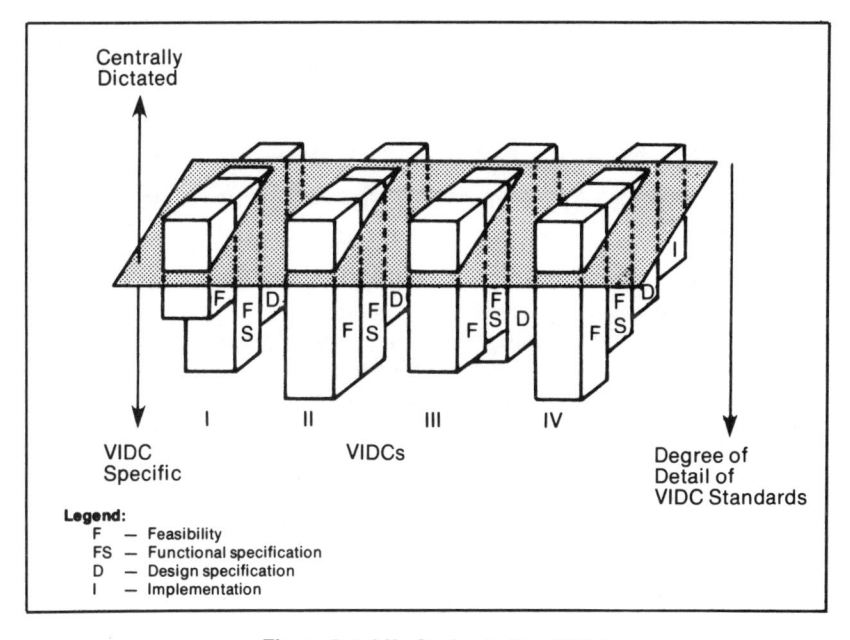

Figure 3-5. Life Cycles in Four VIDCs

Since the decentralized units have different degrees of maturity, it may be desirable to impose different degrees of central control on them. Figure 3-6 illustrates this. Such a scheme, involving varying degrees of autonomy for different organizational units, is complex and difficult to implement.

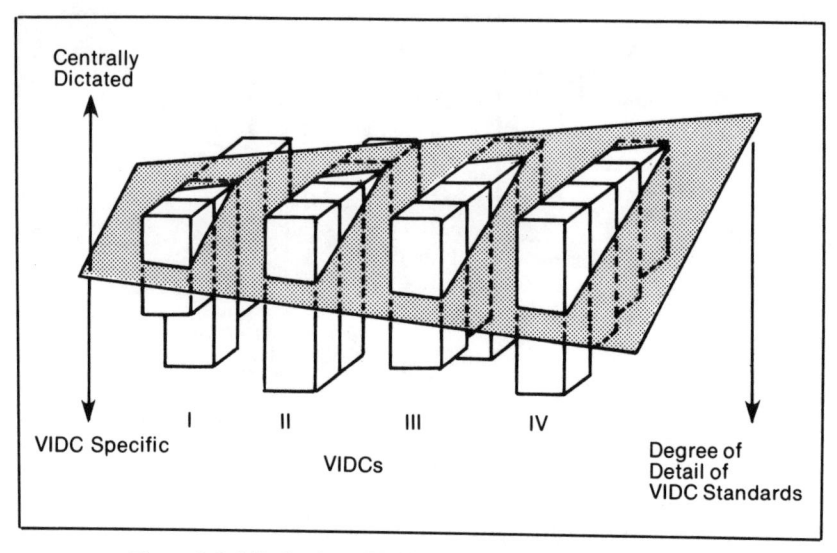

Figure 3-6. Life Cycles with Varying Levels of Central Control

The preceding discussion illustrates the implementation of a single policy regarding project life cycle. Each significant policy must be addressed in a similar manner, clearly specifying the minimum central requirements, the responsibility for adhering to those requirements, and the responsibility and authority for further specification at the local level.

A CORPORATE STAFF FUNCTION FOR POLICIES AND PROCEDURES

In a centralized environment, it is relatively easy for senior management to maintain, interpret, and enforce policies. In the larger, decentralized environment, additional layers of management have been added, and senior management can no longer enforce all policies directly. The only effective alternative to very strong central control over the decentralized units is a staff function responsible for monitoring adherence to policies. Without it, control will be lost.

This staff group has three major responsibilities. First, it must understand the current organization and environment, including everything from new programming techniques and technologies to new market influences. Continual reevaluation of policies is required.

Second, the group must determine which policies, standards, and procedures should be centrally specified and which should be left to the discretion of the decentralized units.

A third function is to develop formal instruction on policies, standards, and procedures and to provide consultation on their correct application. This consultation may be performed by request of the DP units or by management fiat if it becomes clear that a particular policy is not being followed.

ESTABLISHING CONTROLS

In addition to these functions, the staff group should serve as a liaison with other policymaking units in the organization, including higher levels of management and the auditors.

Staffing

To keep current with the changing environment, the staff function should include line personnel chosen on a rotating basis. Serving on this group should be viewed as a choice assignment. Line personnel on their way to higher-level positions should be assigned to this group for a short (one- to two-year) period.

To keep the group small (thereby keeping overhead expense down), resources from outside the group must be used. Internal auditors and managers of the decentralized units are the primary information resources. The group should also have access to the resources of the writing/editing and WP sections.

STANDARDS

Standards take on new importance in a decentralized computing environment. In a mature DP organization, the basic standards for measurement and control should already be in place. New standards must be added to this base to ensure control of decentralization. Standardization must support the organizational objectives that led to decentralization in the first place. It is possible to overstandardize, producing so much "red tape" and overhead that nothing is accomplished. This works against the objective of establishing a more responsive environment. Conversely, very lax standards permit or even encourage divergent efforts and excess costs, working against overall corporate strategies and cost objectives.

The following categories of standards should be considered in a decentralized computing environment:
- Communications
- Systems development
- Data base
- Hardware
- Risk management
- Human resources

Communications

One distinct advantage of a centralized environment is that communications among business applications is greatly simplified. As DP is decentralized, the problems of communications increase. The necessity for horizontal interaction among applications can never be completely eliminated because of requirements for management information and for support of customer needs that cut across the vertical structure. This is especially true in service industries such as banking, where information is the product.

Because communications requires specialized technology and people, MHT created a central group to provide voice and data communications for the business and DP units. This group is responsible for defining and implementing a global communications strategy for the corporation. With the participation of the DP organizations, basic standards have evolved in the following areas:

- Common message header—This is a standard "envelope" that enables the communications network to deliver a message without processing its contents. Within the VIDCs, common formats have been developed to facilitate message processing between external industry networks and internal transaction processing systems. These formats, however, are not defined or enforced at the corporate level.
- Message integrity protocol—Because hardware and communications software may differ from one VIDC to another, a control procedure must be established to reconcile messages sent and received as well as to determine application responsibility during recovery and restart.
- Bulk data transmission—This protocol facilitates the interchange of files among data centers, without incurring the physical preparation and handling of magnetic tapes.

These standards enable the application development organizations to maintain a relatively constant interface to the external world while concentrating on solving business problems.

Systems Development

When systems development was managed centrally by a single manager responsible for all systems and planning activities, it was relatively simple to set standards to control the work process (e.g., standard formats and content for life cycle documents, language conventions, quality reviews, and standards on use of resources). It was often difficult, however, to enforce these centrally defined standards because of the size of the organization and the diversity of applications involved. Thus, decentralized control is beneficial in this area.

Software Package Acquisition. As the use of packaged software increases because of long lead times and lack of development staff, some control and reporting are desirable in the following areas:

- Package evaluation—A central group can establish standard checklists for package evaluation and provide a means for documenting and cataloging the evaluation so that other areas can benefit from the work performed.
- Software package contract negotiation—A central group can perform credit checks and ensure that contracts protect the overall interests of the organization. This group also negotiates quantity discounts and ensures that all provisions of the contract are carried out.

Consultants. The use of consultants to supplement in-house staff is on the rise. A central group should oversee the use of consultants. This group should

ESTABLISHING CONTROLS 43

monitor financial arrangements to obtain the best price for the necessary skills and should control the number of consultants used to ensure adequate career opportunities for the in-house staff and to control project costs. At MHT, the standard states that no more than 20 percent of the development staff can be outsiders. Variances from this guideline are brought to the attention of senior management.

Project Methodology. The project life cycle methodology has been used at MHT for many years. Like the scientific method, it is a logical approach to systems development that is inviolate. The life cycle specifies roles and responsibilities during each of the phases as well as approvals that must be obtained. The content of each phase must be permitted to change based on the technology involved and the maturity of a decentralized unit. For example, a data base might require a conceptual, logical, and physical design, while a non-data-base project might not. Another example is the use of HIPO diagrams rather than narratives for system specifications.

Some degree of flexibility is needed at the local level; however, there are minimum requirements for control and auditability at higher levels. For example, controls, backup and recovery, and data base content sections must be included in the documentation for all projects.

Data Base

In the advanced stages of organizational growth, the value of information as a corporate resource is recognized, and policy statements regarding its acquisition, use, and storage are formulated as they are for other corporate assets or resources. The need to control change and to offer many "views" of data to satisfy divergent user and customer needs requires the use of data base technology. MHT's policy requires the use of a particular data base management system to optimize the use of scarce resources while facilitating the interchange of data between organizational units. Standards for the data dictionary and for the responsibilities of the data base administration function within each VIDC are being evolved on a cooperative basis by the VIDCs. This activity will eventually reach the corporate level after a thorough understanding of the technology and its impact on the business planning process is gained; in the meantime, there is a need to maintain data base activity within each VIDC while not precluding long-term options for integration.

Hardware

In the past, each major development area performed regular hardware evaluations to select equipment to meet the needs of a particular application. Since hardware costs are rapidly declining, it is no longer necessary to optimize a hardware configuration at the expense of software development. Indeed, MHT's current investment in existing software and trained staff exceeds $100 million, therefore, management must formulate policies to protect this investment. In some cases this requires a preferred vendor policy that may be suboptimal for a particular application or user. From a corporate viewpoint, however, the policy is needed to ensure the availability of systems and staff in normal and contingency conditions.

A central authority must review hardware acquisitions to ensure that they are compatible with the corporation's overall goals and strategies. These reviews are only needed for mainframe acquisitions; any system with a purchase price less than $50,000 (including hardware and software) can be selected at the user level, since such systems are viewed as meeting a limited local need.

All installed hardware is controlled and budgeted by the VIDC manager, who is also responsible for overall system performance, unit costs, and control of excess capacity. The VIDC manager reports variances from plans to the central group.

Risk Management

As the decentralized environment evolved, it quickly became apparent that the development of security procedures and contingency plans was taking a back seat to production. The traditional DP approach was oriented to protecting a very expensive hardware asset. Management soon realized, however, that people and software also require protection from loss or compromise.

A risk management group was formed outside of the DP organization to develop top-down policies and procedures relating to exposure control, security, and contingency. This group is responsible for establishing a data base of actual or potential losses that will be used in a risk assessment program to determine the costs of exposure to certain types of losses (e.g., fire, flood, power failure) and to compare these costs with the cost of preventive measures.

This risk management group also has dotted-line authority over security administrators who are responsible for physical security and system security within each data center. Security structures, codes, and programming are developed separately from the systems development activity and under the direction of the security administrator.

Working closely with the various users, DP units, and data administrators, the risk management group is also responsible for policies related to data base use and security and for defining the roles, responsibilities, and authority of owners, users, and custodians of data. Eventually, a specific executive will be made responsible for planning and controlling data base use, access, and integrity.

Human Resources

Because the care and feeding of DP professionals has always required practices and procedures different from those established for the line organizations, MHT created a dedicated DP human resources department attached

ESTABLISHING CONTROLS 45

to the centralized DP organization. This department has responsibility for personnel development, resource planning, and recruiting. In the decentralized organization, personnel liaisons or human resource advisors are assigned to each VIDC to facilitate the use of these central services while focusing on the unique needs of each VIDC.

The central human resources department ensures consistency among the decentralized areas and provides many services, including salary administration, education, and career development.

Salary Administration. Guidelines have been developed to provide equitable salaries based on skill level and measures of performance. These guidelines are monitored to keep MHT competitive with the marketplace.

Education. Customized educational programs are developed to meet the needs of the organization and the employee at a reduced cost. The education program plays a key role in retaining staff and building skills that are not readily available.

Career Development. Career development ensures consistent feedback to the employees while providing them the opportunity to formulate job programs or educational plans to further their professional growth. A mobility program allows horizontal movement within the organization at the request of an individual or of a manager who wishes to "draft" an employee from another division.

IMPLEMENTATION

Without a viable implementation strategy, carefully developed policies and procedures may fail. When implementing policies—especially in a decentralized environment—the following influences must be considered:
- Organizational structure
- Cost
- Availability of capable people
- Management receptivity
- Management philosophy and organizational posture

Organizational Structure

The structure of the organization may dictate where a new policy or procedure is first installed and the amount of "pilot testing" required. In an organization comprised of small compartmentalized units, it is easy to identify and select an appropriate unit in which to start. In fact, it may be productive to install the new process in several units for the sake of comparison.

Cost

The cost (primarily for labor) of monitoring compliance with a proposed policy or procedure is an important consideration. Well before implementation, senior management should be aware of costs and should determine whether the benefits of the policy or procedure justify these costs.

If the monitoring cost is small, demonstrating the value and "functionality" of the procedure is not crucial; if the cost is high, the procedure must be well tested before it is put into general use.

Availability of People

Qualified people must be available to administer the policies and procedures. Without effective administration, procedures can have the opposite of the desired effect. For example, if a central data base administration function is given responsibility to implement procedures under a broad data base policy, the absence of a qualified person would doom the effort to failure and would probably cause regression in data base use.

Management Receptivity

Management support is the single most important factor affecting the success of any policy or procedure, and the level of support given depends upon management's recognition of the need for governing policies and procedures. Therefore, an educational effort is required to ensure management receptivity.

Management Philosophy and Organizational Posture

The philosophy of the DP executive, and of his superiors, will have an enormous impact on the implementation of policies and procedures. In addition, the posture of an organization—its general attitudes and qualities, its stability, the emphasis on control or quality, the degree of willingness to take risks to achieve desired ends, the ease with which change is accepted—affects management's ability to introduce new procedures or standards. If an organization's resistance to change, for instance, is not taken into account and counteracted with adequate training, testing, and gradual implementation, success is unlikely.

Approaches

Policies and procedures must not be implemented on a "one shot" basis; they must be supported with ongoing education and training. If the organization and environment were static, one-time installation might be successful. In the real world, however, changes in personnel, organization, and priorities necessitate continual updating and reinforcement of policies and procedures.

One strategy that has worked well at MHT is implementing a central standard and assigning a dedicated staff to ensure that the standard works. After the initial shakeout period, staff and responsibility for ongoing support of policy can be decentralized.

Another strategy that has proven successful is installing a standard in a decentralized unit on a pilot basis. Given the differing rates of maturation of the decentralized units, it is likely that one unit will be ready for a particular set of standards (e.g., in data base administration) before the others. The standards can be developed and installed in that unit and then fine-tuned through use. Once the standards are working well, they can be transferred to other units as needed. Those portions of the standard that are applicable across the board can be implemented as central standards.

CONCLUSION

In the past, the business planning process and the information system planning process have been separate. As organizations develop, however, they become increasingly dependent on information. Especially in service industries, information is recognized as a valuable "product." Because information systems are beginning to have a direct impact on customer relationships and the bottom line, business and information system strategies *must* be integrated.

Business strategy must recognize information systems as a business investment and provide for end-to-end development and delivery of information to specific market segments. At MHT this is accomplished through the decentralized or vertical organization. MHT has also realized that certain objectives can only be satisfied by integrating efforts horizontally to meet marketplace needs and management information requirements.

Using Nolan's stage hypothesis [1, 2] and the strategy of vertical integration by market segment, the following conclusions can be drawn:
- It is impossible to optimize simultaneously on the horizontal and vertical planes; some suboptimization will occur. MHT decided that it is more desirable to optimize service to the customer.
- Standards should be in place before decentralizing; this facilitates horizontal control. Feedback mechanisms must be in place to prevent "regression" and to avoid having to relearn old lessons.
- DP functions can be decentralized in a controlled manner by developing a pilot function under central control, making corrections and modifications, and then decentralizing the entire structure when success criteria have been met.
- Because the objective of decentralization is ultimately to integrate business and system planning, the process will be governed by the level of learning of the participants (i.e., users, DP personnel, or customers). All parties must grow and mature. This will inevitably create differences among organizational units that will make horizontal coordination more difficult.
- "Push pull" forces will determine the timing and placement of certain functions. Functions existing at higher levels (e.g., financial planning) will be pushed down and decentralized, depending on the maturity of the receiving unit(s). Other functions (e.g., data base administration) will be pulled upward as the need for intraorganizational coordination is recognized by corporate management. Obviously, a function must be

well established in the subordinate units before it is pulled up to the corporate level.
- A dedicated staff group is needed to develop, interpret, educate, and install policies and procedures affecting the decentralized units.
- As the integration of DP, bank operations, and product management activities continues, management will evolve from single-minded profession-oriented thinking to a more generalized business mentality. Interpersonal, team-building, and conflict-resolution skills will be sorely needed, and the human resources organization will play a key role in providing the necessary training and development programs.

References

1. Nolan, Richard L. "Managing the Crisis in Data Processing." *Harvard Business Review*, Vol. 57, No. 2 (March–April 1979), 115–26.
2. Nolan, Richard L. "Restructuring the Data Processing Organization for Data Resource Management." *Information Processing 77: Proceedings of IFIP Congress 77*, Toronto, 1977.

4 Planned Migration to Distributed Systems

by Grayce M. Booth

INTRODUCTION

Some organizations move into DDP by implementing new, "freestanding" applications not previously computerized—for example, installing an integrated patient monitoring/accounting system in a hospital. In such cases, migration problems, from the DP point of view, are nonexistent. In contrast, when a distributed system is implemented by expanding existing computerized applications, several migration concerns arise. This chapter discusses the concerns involved when the decision is made to migrate to DDP and emphasizes the importance of migration planning to a successful DDP implementation.

POTENTIAL MIGRATION IMPACT AREAS

Several areas may be affected by the migration to DDP. Although not all are germane to every distributed system, each area should be studied for potential problems and evaluated for its impact on total DDP planning.

Application Program Change

A move to DDP often means that application-related functions formerly performed by a central host computer are distributed to components located near the users. Many organizations move the control of data entry, including screen forms control and input data editing, to intelligent remote devices as a first step in DDP migration.

Although it is less common, the partitioning of application functions onto remote satellite processors is becoming an increasingly important consideration in migration planning. For example, all processing necessary to handle data flow within a distribution warehouse might be moved from a central computer to a satellite processor at each warehouse. These processors, placed at or near the locations where real-world transactions occur, may be either minicomputers or smaller versions of the general-purpose host computers (e.g., an IBM 4331 used as a satellite processor with an IBM 370 or 303x host).

The *key migration concern* is to ensure that the set of application programs are evolved so that functions can be distributed gradually. For example, if satellite processors are to be installed at point-of-transaction locations, they must be installed individually at the desired locations (see Figure 4-1). As each new satellite is brought online, the appropriate application functions must be deactivated at the host and activated at the satellite location. Throughout the transition phase, the host must continue to support locations where satellite processors are not yet installed. If problems occur at a satellite processor, the necessary host functions must be reactivated to serve that satellite's users until the problems are resolved.

Since each organization and system is unique, specific guidelines cannot be provided for application migration; however, the approach outlined, in which application functions move from a central computer to remote computers, is very common. On the other hand, if the application logic is being changed or expanded significantly at the same time that the functions are being distributed, a more complex situation exists. Here, migration can be eased if the changes are made and/or new functions added to the centralized system before any attempt is made to distribute functions. This practice minimizes the number of simultaneous changes and thus the likelihood that problems will occur.

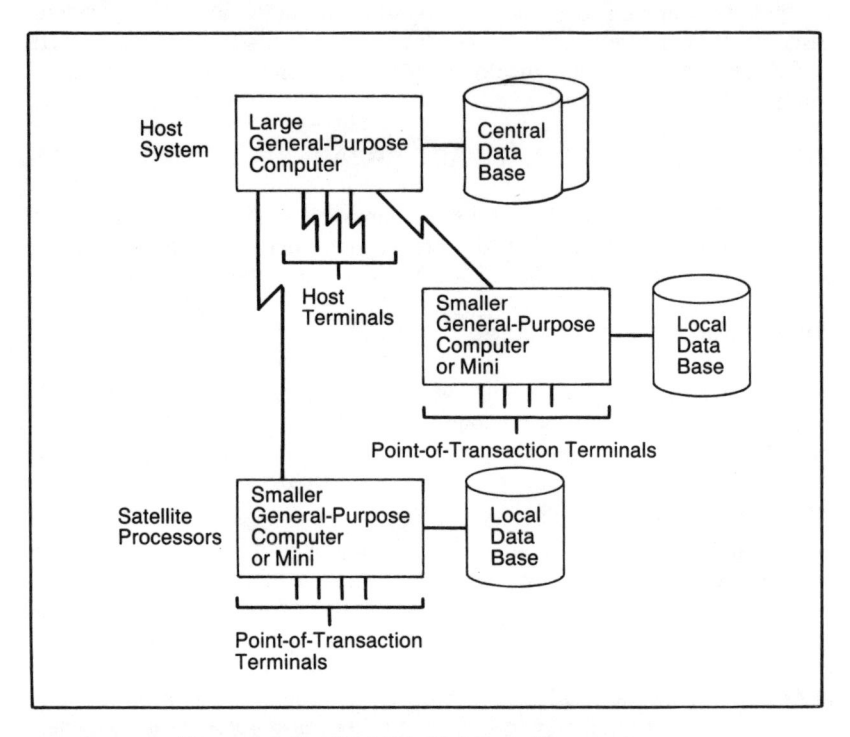

Figure 4-1. Host/Satellite Distributed Processing

System Software Changes

The move to DDP may force changes in the operating system and related software in the host, especially if the reason for migrating to DDP is to change from batch to online processing.

With systems based on IBM equipment, the move to DDP often means a commitment to the Systems Network Architecture (SNA). The adoption of SNA may also involve a change in the telecommunications access method, since only the Virtual Telecommunications Access Method (VTAM) software offers the full range of SNA features. The Telecommunications Access Method (TCAM) software is an alternate choice, especially for mixed SNA and pre-SNA situations.

When a host(s) supplied by another vendor is used, a comparable software change may be required or desirable to support DDP more fully and automatically.

The key migration concern is to ensure that system software is not changed at the same time that functions are being distributed to remote locations. In general, any necessary changes to the host system software should be made before the other steps in the DDP migration process. After these changes have been completed successfully and the system restabilized, other migration steps will have a firm base upon which to build.

Central Site Hardware Change

Although it is often assumed that distributing functions can reduce the load on the central host system(s), new application functions may actually be added. These additions minimize the probability that the central system hardware complement can be reduced or that processing capacity can be available for new uses.

In addition, the need for more complex host-resident software to control the distributed system may offset the distribution of functions formerly performed by the host. A conversion to SNA and VTAM, for example, usually requires additional real memory in the host and may also require an upgrade of host processing power.

The key migration concern is to ensure that all possible hardware requirements are evaluated and that any necessary central system hardware changes are included in the overall migration plan.

Data Base Change

One of the most complex and risk-prone areas in DDP migration is data base change. Online systems are data base centered (i.e., oriented around access to, and dynamic update of, a data base). Since distributed systems are almost always online, they are also data base centered.

If the data base remains centralized, even though some application functions are distributed, the main migration concern is how to accommodate the transition or parallel period of operation. During this period, remote elements of the systems are progressively phased into operation so that some data base accesses and possibly updates originate at terminals attached to remote processors, while others originate at local terminals connected to the host.

It may be appropriate to consider the establishment of a working file(s) containing the portion(s) of the data base modified during the phase-in of remote operations. If the new remote application programs update a working file rather than the main data base, problems can be corrected at the local level before the main data base is updated. The main data base can then be updated at night, when the online part of the system is inactive or activity low.

If portions of the data base are to be distributed, similar transition problems can occur.

If the approach chosen is to selectively copy (replicate) data from the central data base at the satellite processors, the satellite data can again be considered a working file, backed up by the master data base at the host (see Figure 4-2). Of course, the replicated copies must be brought into agreement; this process is often called data base synchronization. Because the replicated data base approach presents the fewest problems with migration, it is currently a popular approach to data base distribution.

If the approach chosen for data base distribution is to partition the data base into nonredundant segments, the migration process may be very complex (see Figure 4-3). If these partitions are split from an existing data base, a copy of the data at the original location should probably be retained until the parallel period is completed and should then be eliminated in favor of the new copy. This is still basically a working file approach.

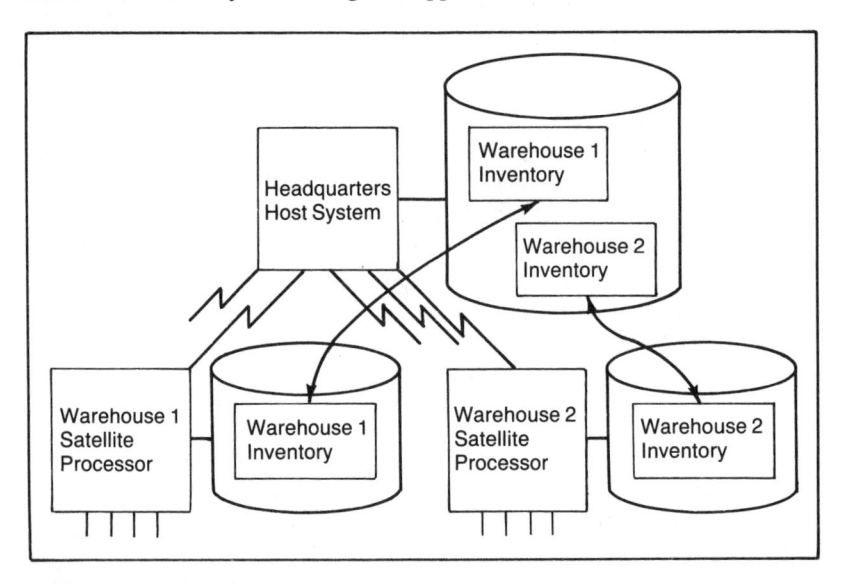

Figure 4-2. Replicated Data Base with Backup

PLANNED MIGRATION

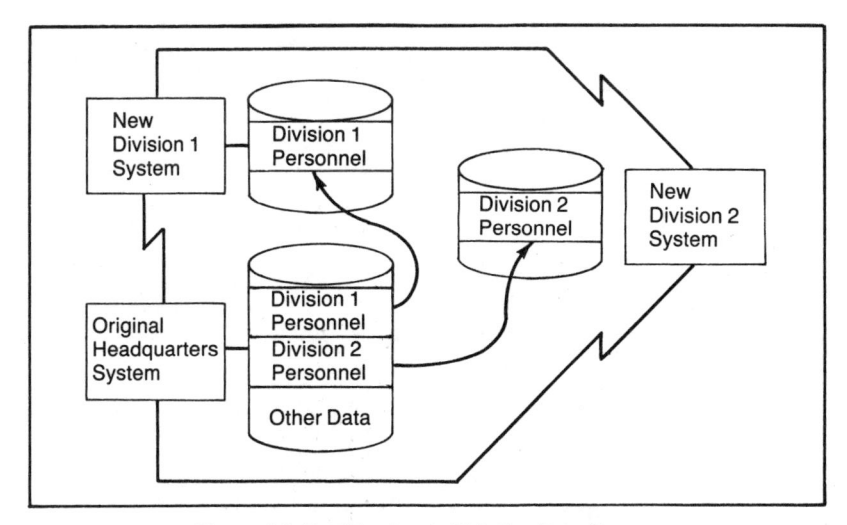

Figure 4-3. Partitioning an Existing Data Base

During the DDP migration, if a partitioned data base is created with new (not previously computerized) data, it is difficult to provide a data base fallback procedure. On the other hand, fallback may be unnecessary. For example, if problems arise at the new remote locations, it may be easier to fall back to manual procedures.

Any of these data base migration approaches can generate a requirement for additional disk storage at the central site. These requirements must be analyzed carefully to ensure that adequate hardware is available, while avoiding, if possible, the installation of additional equipment to meet a temporary need.

The key migration concern is to ensure that data base integrity is not compromised during the transition to DDP.

Communications Network Change

If the evolution to DDP is accompanied by a movement of application processing from batch to online, the requirement is essentially to install a new network. In this case, there are few, if any, migration considerations.

If, however, a network exists before the move to DDP, it must be developed to support the new requirements. For example, terminals previously connected to the central site may now require reconnection to a local processor. These connections may change from data communications links (telephone lines) to direct cable hookups (see Figure 4-4). DDP may also require the installation of additional terminals and/or links to take advantage of new application functions.

Migration problems in the network can generally be minimized by installing any required additional facilities in advance. This allows a cushion of extra time should installation delays occur.

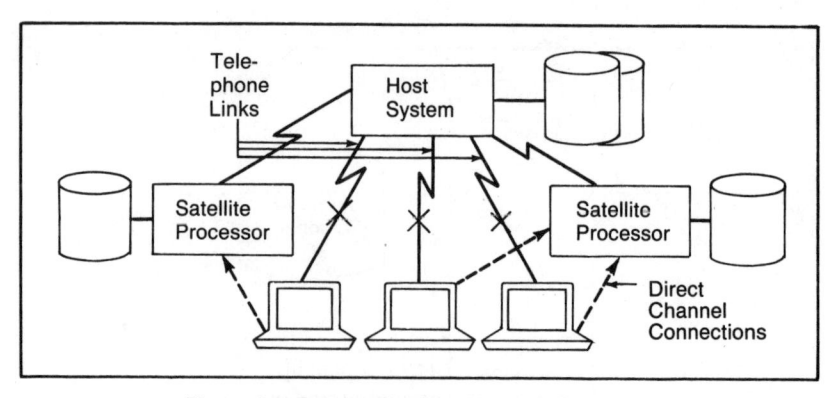

Figure 4-4. Communications Network Change

If feasible, changes in network connections should be temporary so that if problems arise, the original network connections can be restored. Unfortunately, this is often difficult, especially without incurring significantly higher costs.

When faced with a complex situation, such as moving existing terminals from host connections to local satellite processors while distributing formerly centralized functions, the best plan is to localize the transition efforts. A satellite processor should be installed at, or very near, the central computer site, with one set of terminals connected to the satellite processor. Alternate connections for switching back to the host should be retained, preferably though patch panel for quick changes. Finally, all aspects of the new system should be thoroughly tested with this processor and set of terminals. When this shakedown period is completed, the satellite processor can be moved to the desired remote location and its terminals switched over.

In an extremely complex system, this process should be repeated until two or three remote locations have been installed successfully. With that experience it should then be possible to cut over the remaining locations, with a high probability of success. This approach minimizes the need to install backup connections as terminals are cut over from the host to the new local processors. It also allows the first cut-overs to occur at the central site, which is usually located near the design and implementation staff. The logistics problems often encountered in debugging a complex system at multiple, geographically dispersed locations are also minimized.

The key migration concern is to plan installation and cut-over with minimal switching between the old and new network connections.

Satellite Processors

The move to DDP often involves a decision to use satellite processors close to the point-of-transaction locations. Application-related functions and possibly a segment of the data base are distributed to each satellite.

PLANNED MIGRATION

If satellite processors are being installed for the first time, there are no migration concerns associated with the satellite itself but rather with the surrounding environment—the host, network, and terminals.

If existing satellite processors are being modified or expanded, the key migration concerns that apply to the host must also be analyzed. These include changes to application programs, system software, hardware, and the data base.

Terminal Device Change

Changes at the terminal level may involve adding new features to expand the capabilities of existing terminals or replacing them with new types of terminals. In the former case, the key migration concern is to ensure that the new features are ordered in ample time for installation.

Terminal devices may be replaced if the existing devices have limited expansion capability or are incompatible with the remainder of the new DDP equipment. If the new devices are upward compatible with current devices, the migration process should be straightforward. If, however, devices that are incompatible in terms of communications protocol are used, migration must be carefully planned.

A lengthy period in which both the old and new terminals are installed would be difficult and costly, especially if private communications links are used and incompatibility forces the use of separate links for the old and new devices. The key migration concern, therefore, is to ensure that the transition period is as short as possible. The best approach is the technique outlined in the Communications Network Change section. The first of the new devices should be installed in or near the central computer site. All necessary testing should be performed to ensure that the terminals can be converted successfully before actually moving the new equipment to the first remote locations. Subsequent switch-overs at additional sites should then be trouble free.

Terminal Use Procedure Changes

Successful DDP migration depends on well-designed procedures for users of terminals. If the move to DDP involves changes in existing methods, they must be included in migration planning.

The key migration concern here is to ensure that users are involved in every phase of the planning for the new procedures and interfaces. Of course, not all users can be involved in the planning; however, as many users as possible should be encouraged to participate.

All users must be trained in the new methods before cut-over begins. Informal sessions, in which all users have an opportunity to use the new procedures on real terminals, are the most successful form of training. Although this level of training may be expensive, it minimizes the potentially costly problems associated with inadequate training and/or negative attitudes.

Operational Procedure Changes

Many current computer systems operate under control of the console operators at the central site, even when telephone lines and remote terminals are involved. In online systems, this can create problems because the central-site operators must keep the central-site equipment operating properly as well as resolve problems in the network or at terminal locations.

As the complexity of online systems increases, a trend toward a system administration staff (also called a network control staff) is emerging to cope with problems that occur away from the central site. For example, if a terminal user at a remote location receives erroneous data or cannot contact the central site, the system administration staff must take appropriate action. Often, this includes using diagnostic programs and/or communications link analysis devices that can pinpoint the source of the problem, whether it be the communications link, the terminal device, the modem(s), or the central site equipment. Once the origin of the problem is located, the appropriate service engineer(s) from the telephone company, the terminal vendor, and/or the computer vendor can be called to correct the difficulty.

The key migration concern is to ensure that a system administration function is established well in advance of the move to DDP. Personnel should be selected, hired, and trained; diagnostic equipment should be acquired; and the staff should be thoroughly familiar with the DDP system goals and design. Since the system administration staff makes decisions that affect the operation of the system and thus of the business or enterprise that the system supports, they must fully understand the effects of their decisions and how these decisions will be viewed by management.

PREFERRED APPROACHES TO MIGRATION

The following rules are essential for a successful migration to distributed systems.

Adopt a Gradual, "Piece at a Time" Approach. Such an approach allows problems to be localized and corrected before the distributed system is fully implemented. This approach is especially important in geographically dispersed distributed systems. Each office or branch should be installed individually, and cutover at one site should be completed before it begins at another. Of course, in a very large system this approach can be modified after the successful conversion of several locations; multiple sites should then be converted in parallel if the necessary staff resources are available.

The gradual approach should also be considered if the new system involves multiple new functions. If feasible, these functions should be implemented independently so that one can be converted or installed before the other(s) is undertaken. This modular functional migration can be combined with cutover of geographic locations to produce a migration plan for installing successive functions and locations during the cut-over period.

Implement and Test Close to Design Staff. The installation of a distributed system involves many complex problems, some of which relate to the geographical dispersion of terminals and users and possibly of information processing resources as well. If the first installations are at, or near, the central site, the implementation staff need not pack up their entire set of documentation to travel to remote sites. In addition, such placement can eliminate or minimize the problems associated with the communications network, allowing initial focus on the computing logic and terminal procedures. Once these are operating satisfactorily, the move to the first remote site can occur.

In choosing a pattern for migrating sites to DDP, those closest to the offices of the design/implementation staff should be chosen as pilot sites. When these have been installed successfully, the move to more remote locations can begin.

Because the implementation staff will be intimately involved with the installation of the first terminal sites, it is important not to dilute their effectiveness by forcing them to operate in remote locations and cope with multiple variables concurrently. Minimizing the number of problems that can occur simultaneously is a basic rule for success in the implementation of any information system, especially a distributed system.

Train Terminal Users. Another important rule is to train users early in the design of distributed systems. Involving users in the design of terminal use procedures ensures that the system meets their needs and, at the same time, fosters a positive attitude toward the new or changed system.

Provide Contingency Planning. It is essential that all factors are considered in the migration to DDP. Although the degree of complexity depends on the specific design, the migration will never be simple. A well-thought-out plan, which allows ample time for successful parallel operation and cut-over before eliminating old procedures (manual and/or computerized), must be part of the overall DDP migration planning.

Contingencies must also be allowed for in the transition/parallel plan. If unexpected difficulties develop, it must be possible to fall back to an earlier set of conditions while these difficulties are resolved. Migration must allow for fallback to provide adequate support for the organization's functions.

Include Migration Planning in Corporate-wide DDP Planning. Because DDP, like any online system, supports the main operations of the organization, the involvement and support of high-level management are essential.

In addition, the migration to DDP can cause stress during the transition; therefore, all levels of management must be apprised of all operations to gain the full cooperation of all parties in achieving the goals and the benefits of the new distributed system.

5 Designing the User System in a Distributed Environment

by Joseph Podolsky

INTRODUCTION

The first major distinction between centralized processing and DDP involves the type of work to be accomplished. In centralized processing, characteristics include:
- Work is usually batch oriented.
- Input data is usually edited carefully after the data entry process.
- The work cycle tends to be routine and repetitive.
- Changes to the system must be well documented and approved by many people throughout the corporation.
- The systems tend to be organized around functions (e.g., general accounting, cost accounting, and inventory control) rather than around the needs of a given department or manager.
- Computer processing usually replaces clerical paper processing; any information that is created is a by-product of that processing.
- The system generally uses files that are shared by many applications rather than be restricted to a given function.
- Teleprocessing tends to form star networks.
- The system's capacity is relatively flexible, especially in a multiprocessing environment. The question usually is not whether the job can be accomplished but the length of time needed to do the job.

In contrast, with DDP, the characteristics include:
- The system tends to be online and is often real time. Thus, a terminal is usually involved and perhaps even a dedicated, low-cost standalone computer.
- Each transaction is edited as completely as possible at the time of data entry so that the user can immediately correct the transaction.
- The system can be designed so that it processes transactions on a routine, repetitive basis. DDP systems, however, can also be designed to allow unpredictable inquiries to the data base and often to allow and/ or encourage the use of "quick and dirty" BASIC or RPG programs to meet low-priority, local processing needs.
- Changes can be made to the system with a minimum of approvals and documentation, thus making the system more responsive to changing user needs.

- The system can be designed to perform specific local functions; in addition, it can be (and is more likely to be) tailored to the personal requirements of given users or user departments.
- The system tends to be task oriented, performing work that would otherwise be completed by clerical and/or manual systems operations. By-product information may come from paper reports or from systems that allow online inquiry into specific aspects of the process or data.
- DDP connotes the use of local (i.e., specialized, private) files. These, in turn, may feed into, or be built from, a central file.
- Teleprocessing networks can be designed in many formats. The system can be a star network where all communication is to and from a central site. The system can be a ring network in which each node talks to only specific "neighbor" nodes or can be topological networks in which any node can talk to any other node.
- Because of the capacity limitations of the systems used in DDP, problems may exceed the reasonable capacity of local machines; absolute capability is thus as important in systems design as is responsiveness. DDP systems should often be limited to relatively small tasks.

A second major consideration, in addition to the type of work that must be accomplished, is computer operations. In a centralized environment, the user rarely works directly with the computer but rather with a piece of paper. The paper is submitted to a data entry operator, who then creates a machine-readable format that is entered into the computer.

In a DDP environment, the user typically works with a computer or a terminal that interfaces with a computer. The user must begin to treat that piece of computing hardware as though it were any other tool in an office environment (e.g., a calculator, telephone, filing cabinet, pencil, or paper). The system, therefore, must be suitable for that environment. (One set of criteria that might be used to determine the suitability of such a local system is that the system be small, simple, relatively inexpensive, and friendly [1].)

CHARACTERISTICS OF USER DDP SYSTEMS

To be successful from a user standpoint, a DDP system must meet the user's specialized needs and must be sufficiently flexible to continue to meet the user's needs as they change. In the words of L.E. Donegan:

> The beauty of distributed data processing is the number of times you don't have to say no. It's thrilling. So many times in the past, our job has been learning how to say 'no' to our users. [2]

System Relationships

While a DDP system must serve local needs, it may also have to include certain standard, periodic interfaces with other nodes in a larger system. These nodes and interfaces may be *hierarchical* (summary data is passed to a superior organizational element, and/or more detailed information is passed to

DESIGNING THE USER SYSTEM 61

a subsidiary organizational element) or *peer* (action and/or operational information is passed to "equal" organizational elements). Within these interface boundaries, however, the local manager is allowed and/or encouraged to have the system meet his specific needs.

Within the limits of these interface boundaries, changes can be made to the local system without consulting other organizational elements. These changes can be made as the result of functional differences between organizational elements, or they can reflect the personal styles of the local users. In a DDP environment, systems development will probably be iterative (i.e., a prototype system can be built and used, later to be modified as more information on how the system should function becomes available).

Obviously, certain precautions must be taken when applying these concepts. One must be aware of:
- The frequency of changes required because of user turnover
- Arbitrary rejection of existing systems (perhaps used elsewhere) because of the not-invented-here syndrome
- The loss in capability that results from the fact that the local user is working in relative isolation
- Rapid changes required by growth in a local environment
- A tendency of operational management (and local management is usually operationally oriented) to design systems for short-term needs only
- The lack of appropriate/professional DP expertise

One way to achieve flexibility for local needs and avoid the preceding pitfalls is to utilize a report specifically tailored to the DDP environment. The following report options are available for a DDP environment (these options are also available, to a limited extent, in a centralized environment):
- Reports designed and programmed for local use
- Generalized reporting systems that can be custom-tailored by parameter cards entered locally
- The use of report compilers (e.g., RPG or Mark IV)
- Online inquiry mechanisms that are related to a given data base management system

Types of DDP

Systems designers make many choices in the design of DDP systems that directly affect the user environment, including the following:
- Computing hardware—Should the hardware configuration be decentralized or centralized? Should the system be homogeneous, with all sites having the same computers and terminals, or heterogeneous, with hardware facilities varying among sites?
- Data base design—Should the data base be partitioned, with each local element having exclusive ownership of its own data, or replicated, with each local site having a copy of the data that it needs?
- Data structures—Are the data structures at various sites compatible or noncompatible with each other or with the central facility?

- Software—Are the systems and applications software systems homogeneous (identical at all local sites) or heterogeneous (different at each site)?
- Programming—Are all programmers located at a central facility, or is programming done primarily at local sites?
- Costs—Are the costs for both programming and operations allocated to individual users or absorbed by a centralized DP cost center?
- Maintenance—Are changes to application systems made by the centralized programming staff, or are they done locally?
- Standards—Are standards controlled centrally or defined on a local level?
- Audit—Is the corporation interested in auditing only the results of the local DP efforts, or is the corporation also concerned about the detailed examination of the processes by which those results are obtained?
- Reporting options—Should there be local reports or local inquiry into online data bases?
- Data entry options—Should there be local online data entry or local real-time updating of at least local data bases?

Control

The question of control in a DDP environment is very important. Several areas of systems controls should be considered:

Audit Trails. Audit trails are of particular concern in DDP because the systems often lack the hard-copy visibility that exists in traditional batch systems.

System Backup. As with any DP system, some type of file backup is needed to recover from processing errors that occur in recovering from damage to the local system. A replacement system might also be needed when, for some reason, the primary local system is unavailable.

Adherence to Policies and Procedures. In centralized environments, DP professionals who understand the risks inherent in DP can create the policies and procedures necessary to minimize exposure to those risks. Although these same policies and procedures can be written for a DDP environment, they are not usually enforced as rigorously as in a centralized environment.

Accuracy of Data. Because processing is dispersed in a DDP environment and relatively inexperienced people work directly with machine-readable data, it is possible that transactions are made improperly and that data is incomplete and inaccurate.

Accuracy and Completion of Documentation. The purpose of documentation in a traditional DP environment is to minimize dependence on specific individuals. Accomplishing this in a DDP environment is more difficult because of the geographic dispersion of the sites and the lack of functional specialization and professional training among users.

Less Frequent Audits. Geographic dispersion of sites makes audits more expensive, less frequent, and, therefore, less effective.

Separation of Responsibilities. At local sites, there is usually less separation of key responsibilities; the more functions performed by one individual, the greater the probability of error and other control problems.

Distribution of Changes. If, for example, program changes are made from a central source, it may be several days (or, in some cases, several weeks) before the documentation for those changes is received at all dispersed sites.

Cutoff Times. The control of date and time cutoffs may be harder to implement at all local sites because of time zone differences and/or local practices regarding working hours.

Better control can be achieved through several means:
- All transactions and messages entered into a local terminal or computer should be logged offline (probably on a tape drive); this log then provides the audit trail that can be examined at a later date.
- Controls/audit trails can often be traced to a given terminal. This capability is an advantage that DDP provides auditors. In addition, transactions can be restricted to specific locations.
- When a message is sent from one node to another, some type of acknowledgment should be returned so that the sending location is aware that the transmission has been received.
- The number of messages sent between two sites should be tabulated, and a balancing report should be produced periodically during the day.
- Because audits may be less frequent, the responsibility for control must be clearly assigned to a local line manager.
- In those environments where homogeneous, centralized programming is occurring, consistency can often be achieved by downloading programs from one site to the next. These programs are usually transferred among sites in a machine-readable format.
- Since the documentation of changes in the system is as important as the programs themselves, all documentation in machine-readable format should be transmitted, along with the changes, to the program code.
- Transactions that exist in a local message log should include the transactions made to the data files as well as all commands issued at that local site and the other systems within the network.
- The local systems should contain checkpoint/restart methods to assist recovery in case of systems failure.
- Levels of guidance should be programmed into the system.
- All edits should be performed as closely as possible to the user who initiated the data.

- The systems designers and users must be very conscious of the potential for creating duplicates, especially when transactions have been rejected by the system edits.
- Tests and authorized backup procedures should be established in backup sites should the local system fail.
- Some type of local time reference should be established throughout the corporation. Most often, the time used in DDP is the clock time at the corporate headquarters.
- If job separation is impractical, job rotation may be useful so that different people periodically perform different elements of the overall task.

Security Considerations

Another critical issue in implementing DDP systems is security. DDP systems pose several threats to security:
- The lack of separation among tasks in the user/DP environment invites potential security violations.
- An informal work atmosphere may exist at remote sites, thus preventing strict security discipline from being followed.
- Passwords/security procedures need to be communicated from the central security source to the local site in some way. The process of communication is often subject to some type of security breach.
- The need for local sites to communicate with central and/or local sites in machine-readable format may result in passwords for distant sites being found in a given local site. As a result, a security breach in a given site may compromise the entire network.
- Insurance to compensate the corporation in case of a security violation might be more difficult or more expensive to obtain because of the diverse nature of the remote sites.
- One of the security procedures most likely to be breached at local sites is the intensive screening of all personnel who come in contact with sensitive systems. Because employees in these environments often perform various functions, prospective employees might be selected for reasons other than their ability to use the system correctly at the local site.

Tight security can be ensured in several ways:
- Good security policy and procedures should be written for remote sites, even though people in the remote sites may deviate from them.
- The facility (user) manager, not just DP-related staff, should be made responsible for security.
- Plans should be developed for the security of all transmission (e.g., data, voice, and/or mail) among sites.
- Staff levels, time, and budgets needed to adequately audit remote sites should be established. An audit usually requires a minimum of two visits per year to a remote site.
- The security for any backup files taken from the remote site should be

as carefully considered as is the security of the primary production files.
- Technologically advanced alternatives to passwords should be considered. For example, specially coded magnetic identification cards, voice print identification, encoded read-only memory chips, and finger/handprint devices are becoming sufficiently inexpensive to be considered in selected applications.
- In evaluating technically advanced alternatives, those charged with responsibility for security should not overlook such simple solutions as physically locking the terminals with a key or electronically shutting off remote or dial-up access to a given system.
- Contingency plans must be sufficiently detailed to be usable when an emergency occurs. These plans, however, must also be viewed as a security risk—very often, they provide security information that would otherwise be restricted.
- Consideration must be given to personnel who service and repair the system at remote sites. These people might have access to security information that affects a given remote site as well as other sites in the network.
- Managers must always be conscious of the relative cost and value of the security. This cost/value balance must be carefully weighed, especially in those sites where access is truly available only to local files. Excessive security is costly and discourages appropriate use of the system and eventually *creates* security risks in the form of cynical system users.

System Reliability

The problems associated with system reliability are exacerbated in DDP because of the local users' lack of technical expertise. Hardware and software reliability are essential for any system but are especially crucial in the consideration of distributed systems.

Hardware Reliability. Any device placed in the local environment, whether it is a standalone computer or a terminal, must be constructed so that it operates reliably in the user environment. If that environment is unusual (e.g., dirty, cold, or electrically noisy), the system must be constructed so that it operates under those conditions.

The system hardware must also be safe under a variety of normal conditions. Again, the key consideration is that the user is relatively unsophisticated; thus, he or she should be protected as much as possible from physical dangers (e.g., jagged edges on hardware cabinets) and from electrical dangers (e.g., electrical shock from touching an ungrounded system).

The hardware should be designed and constructed in such a manner that routine maintenance is very straightforward. Those areas of the machine that can be accessed safely by relatively unsophisticated users should be separated from those areas that should be accessed only by well-trained technicians. This prevents harm befalling both user and machine.

When failures do occur, the hardware must be restored to operating condition as quickly as possible without adversely affecting user operations. Thus, modular equipment is necessary because a modular design permits the user to replace an entire unit or major subassembly rather than diagnose failures. When a user must diagnose failures, the procedure should be sufficiently simple that the user can do most of it, or the failure should be capable of being diagnosed remotely. If neither of these options is viable, spare equipment is probably the most cost-effective way of achieving system reliability in remote sites.

Software Reliability. Many of the same precautions taken for hardware also apply with software; in addition, a few specific considerations pertain to the software environment in DDP.

To the extent possible, all reasonable error conditions should be handled within the boundaries of the application program. From the standpoint of an unsophisticated user, when the application program aborts and defaults to the operating system, it is probably a systems failure.

The user should be able to leave a particular screen or system and return to a main menu or some master program from which he can start over. There is nothing more frustrating than being locked into a program, knowing that something is wrong but not knowing how to correct the problem (and not even knowing how to stop the process without creating further damage).

The software should also allow the user to reconstruct data files from the last checkpoint taken and should even allow the user to reconstruct the program if it has been damaged.

Finally, the software should, to the extent possible, allow the diagnosis of any problems that exist within the software. The diagnosis may involve the use of error messages, trace routines, test data sets, and so on. The goal of diagnostic examinations is to allow the user to correct the software faults or to communicate the exact nature of the problem to either local- or central-based experts.

User Training

For adequate user training, there must be three well-planned training procedures:
1. The initial training, which, when the system is first implemented, brings the users onto the system. This training is particularly important because, to some extent, it validates the system; in addition, it provides designers the feedback they need to enhance the system and improve its usefulness.
2. Ongoing/continuing training of users involves the review of existing concepts as well as the introduction of new software or procedural techniques.

3. Informal training is done after the system is successfully operating in a given location. The initial training is usually done by systems experts; informal training is given to new or replacement personnel by operators who may not thoroughly know all aspects of the system. This type of on-the-job training requires special materials and procedures to ensure that it is done correctly.

Most training materials should be clearly identified as either guidance or reference. Guidance materials provide a step-by-step definition of how a given job is done; the classic example of this is the well-known play-script approach to procedure writing. Reference materials, however, are usually composed of topical subjects arranged in some sort of manual, with each subject described in depth; an index is usually provided.

Both types of training materials can be built into a system so that they are available by way of a terminal. Guidance training can be provided by programmed instruction, while reference materials can be made available through a Help command. The use of such computer-aided training, however, makes it even more critical that all materials be updated when the system is modified.

Experienced users tend not to use training material at all; rather, they memorize regularly used procedures and codes. Because of this fact, all changes to the procedures or codes must be flagged to clarify to these users that something has changed. In addition, any procedural and/or code changes that are flagged for the user should be changed in the programs. These changes can prevent incorrect procedures or data from damaging the system. System edits keep inaccurate data from damaging the system and also provide the user with negative reinforcement, thus training the user to avoid errors in the future.

Communications among Locations

The user system should differentiate between hierarchical and peer communications.

In hierarchical processing, the detail operational transaction processing is usually done at the lowest level of the organization; detail and summary information is a by-product of this processing. This information is then transmitted to other organizational levels, where the summaries become local files. At that organizational level, the local computer can process these sets of data to produce reports or allow inquiries. Depending on the number of levels in the hierarchy, these steps can occur several times. Progressive summaries are usually much less detailed, further removed from the real-time processing of the transactions (in fact, they are usually based on some accounting time period), and more amenable to economical batch processing.

While hierarchical processing is usually viewed from the bottom up, there is no reason to limit the flow to that direction only; in fact, data can be transmitted from a higher to a lower organizational level. This approach is typical in such top-down situations as planning and financial targeting.

The transmission of data among peer organizational elements usually involves operational data that is sent to another location for information or action. For example, an order may be placed at one sales office by a customer's central headquarters; however, because the order involves customer branches located throughout the country, specific parts of the order must be transmitted to local sales offices that can serve the local customers.

Regardless of the type of communications and the level of detail of the data, three procedural steps should be built into the system to allow communications to occur:

1. The recipient of the data should have some means to acknowledge that a complete transmission has been received; this can often be done as part of the network transmission software protocol.
2. The recipient must, from a "data logic" standpoint, accept or reject the contents of the transmission. If, for example, a sales order has been sent from one sales office to another in a peer transmission, the receiving sales office must be able to say, Yes, it is appropriate that I have this transaction or No, it's not mine. Likewise, when data flows up a hierarchy, a way must exist for the next level to say, Yes, I received all the data, but for some reason, I believe it could be incomplete or incorrect, so please send me corrections so that the data can be processed at this next level.
3. There must be a mechanism by which any disputes between the sender and the recipient can be arbitrated. In the preceding sales example, if one sales office manager denies responsibility for the sales order, there must be some mechanism by which the sender, the receiver, or both can refer to a higher authority who can determine at what location the sales order should be processed. This arbitration procedure should be an integral part of the DDP system.

Cost Considerations

Although DDP might be more costly from a unit-cost standpoint, it does provide economies of specialization. In general, the cost savings realized with DDP accrue directly to the users rather than to any DP organization.

One savings that users experience is a shorter lead time between the statement of the problem and (at least) a preliminary solution. Very little loss is experienced in translating the requirement from the user to the DP specialist; in fact, the user often does not have a DP specialist and develops the system on local hardware by himself. In addition, because users design their own systems to meet their own needs, the compromises and overhead cost associated with generalized systems are eliminated.

For operational systems, responsiveness can be much more immediate than in a centralized system. Because the user does not have to await his results, presumably his productivity is much higher. Because DDP usually involves online inquiry, there is no need to produce costly reports in which only a few lines are actually used in a given day.

DESIGNING THE USER SYSTEM

TECHNICAL SUPPORT

The types of local support needed in DDP systems are discussed in the following sections.

Local Systems Manager. Each local site must have one person who is responsible for both hardware and software in the local system. This person is not necessarily the users' direct supervisor; he or she must be someone whose authority in technical matters will be respected.

This person:
- Acts as a conduit for all communication between the local site and other sites in the distributed network
- Guides local users on how the system should be used in the specific environment
- Assumes responsibility for the capacity and the capability of the local hardware and software and recommends changes in system configuration
- Assumes responsibility for the housekeeping tasks of the local site, including user training, control backup, and security

Local Technical Reference. This person may be either the systems manager or a user who completely understands the hardware and systems software at the local site. This individual is a local version of the operations manager and systems programmer often found on larger central sites. The local technical reference may, in fact, cover several physical sites in the network; however, the key to his effectiveness is his ready (within a few hours) availability to any given site.

The local technical reference should:
- Be knowledgeable in hardware and systems software so that in case of failure, he would know to call either a customer engineer (for hardware failures) or the central software expert (for systems software failures)
- Suggest ways of improving the performance (efficiency) of the hardware and software systems and perhaps even make local changes to optimize processing on the local system
- Be available to install additional terminals or other new pieces of hardware or to apply updates to systems software
- Advise on hardware/software installation and layout
- Advise and train on hardware operations
- Advise on the appropriate procedures for system security and backup (although the systems manager should be responsible for ensuring that the suggested procedures are carried out)

Operator/User Backup. In order to maintain a reliable operation, at least two people should be able to perform every task associated with the DDP system. To accomplish this:
- Good training documentation must be available.
- Training must be available on both a continuing basis and for new employees.

- Personnel designated as either primary or backup must be allowed to perform the actual work periodically to reinforce their training.
- Both the primary and backup personnel must receive all ongoing documentation and updates.
- The local systems manager must coordinate the activities and schedules of the primary and backup personnel to ensure that both are not away at the same time. He must also ensure that as turnover occurs, both a primary and a backup person have been designated and trained.

In addition to local support, the central facility should provide in-depth backup to the local experts just described. The same functions must be provided with a greater scope and depth of understanding in case of problems. This support can be provided in many ways, including those discussed in the following sections.

Telephone Consulting. The central facility should provide a phone-in consulting service by which the local person (ideally, the local systems manager or the local technical reference—not the user) can get advice and/or aid when problems cannot be solved locally.

Visits by the Central Experts. These visits often benefit the central experts more than they benefit the local sites and put the experts into touch with the situation at the local sites. The visiting experts also communicate information generated at the central site to local sites and communicate good operating ideas generated at one site to all other sites.

The visiting experts can also provide an important social link among the various distributed sites, especially if they are widely dispersed. Personnel who perform the same functions at the various sites have probably talked with each other on the telephone but only have vague impressions about the personal characteristics of each other. The visiting experts can often provide informal-type information that allows the interpersonal relations to proceed much more smoothly. (It has been suggested that the local experts take photographs of key people at various sites and distribute those photographs among the sites.)

The visitors should always provide feedback to personnel at the local sites. The purpose of the feedback is to share information as well as to give the people at the local sites a feeling that they are an integral part of the entire corporate network.

It is often helpful to have users visit sister sites. Because of the expense involved, these visits are usually infrequent; however, to the extent that they do occur, they can:
- Produce cross-training and cross-fertilization of ideas
- Provide insight about future changes in personnel assignments among sites
- Because of the informal contacts established during a visit, establish better working relationships among geographically dispersed locations

DESIGNING THE USER SYSTEM

A less expensive (but less effective) alternative to intersite visits is to hold a users conference at a central location. Although this alternative allows some information to be transferred among users and fosters some interpersonal contact, it does not allow the users to see each other in their work environment; thus, subtle elements of information may, in fact, not be transferred.

CONCLUSION

The user is the critical element in DDP because it is the user who will obtain whatever benefits accrue from DDP. In fact, from a strict economical and technical viewpoint, DDP is probably less effective than is centralized DP; thus, it is important that the user be considered in all elements of the design of the DDP network and that everything be done to ensure that the potential benefits are realized.

References

1. E.F. Shumacker. *Small is Beautiful: A Study of Economics as if People Mattered.* London: Abacus, 1974.
2. L.E. Donegan. Quoted within an advertisement prepared by International Data Corporation and published in *Fortune* (June 1979), 23.

6 User Chargeback Procedures for Distributed Systems

by William E. Perry

INTRODUCTION

During the late 1950s and early 1960s, few organizations charged users for DP services. Computer concepts were new and unproven, and the primary challenge was to make systems work. In addition, a computer was frequently viewed as a status symbol. These conditions made recouping costs from users seem unimportant.

Users soon began to recognize the great potential of the computer and to request more computerized functions. This desire for expanded computerization was fueled by the fact that DP services were free. In an attempt to make users accountable for their computerized applications, many organizations directed their DP departments to charge back costs to the users. This made it necessary for each user to justify his DP expenditures in the departmental budget.

In many organizations chargeback procedures had a negative effect. One initial result was a drastic curtailment of computerization. Another negative effect was the extra effort expended in designing systems solely to minimize chargeback costs. For example, if an organization charged a user for services based on the number of lines printed, systems were designed to consume more computer time while decreasing the number of lines printed. On the other hand, if an organization's basis for chargeback was the number of CPU minutes consumed, systems often included procedures for printing hundreds of thousands of lines of data offline while reducing the CPU minutes consumed.

Too many chargeback systems were thus developed without sufficiently considering the impact of these chargeback procedures. Organizations currently moving into the DDP environment should learn from past mistakes, however, and develop chargeback procedures designed to meet management objectives. This requires developing a DDP strategy and then developing a chargeback procedure to support that strategy.

Objectives of Chargeback Procedures

There are as many variations of chargeback procedures as there are organizations developing them. These procedures are usually developed with the assistance of accountants to ensure that the procedures fit into the accounting structure of the organization. In developing the procedures, the following factors should be considered:
- Expense—Chargeback procedures should be inexpensive to design, implement, and operate. A chargeback procedure is a tool for increasing management control of the use of computer resources. A control tool should not cost more than the expenditures it is designed to prevent. If chargeback procedures become too cumbersome and complex, the time and effort expended to implement them may exceed their value.
- Ease of use—The procedures for preparing data for a chargeback system should not consume much effort. When DP personnel are required to maintain elaborate time-reporting systems, the chargeback system often breaks down because people fail to devote the time necessary to record the required information.
- Accuracy—The information gathered from chargeback procedures should accurately represent the resources actually expended. This is one of the more difficult aspects of designing chargeback procedures because people are reluctant to report information that may have a negative impact on their performance evaluations. Thus, the procedures should be designed to collect data solely for chargeback purposes rather than for performance appraisals.
- Readily understandable reports—The information provided through chargeback procedures should be easy to understand. If people need to study the reports in order to understand the meaning of the chargeback information, the value of the information will be limited.
- Automated collection—As much chargeback information as is practical should be gathered through automated processes. For example, job accounting systems have proved very effective in gathering operational chargeback information. The ideal chargeback system would gather all information as a by-product of various DP systems.

Approaches for Designing User Chargeback Procedures

Chargeback procedures provide management with a tool for influencing user decisions about distributed processing. Planners developing the chargeback procedures should therefore decide how the procedures will help in achieving management objectives, and top management should play a role in selecting the chargeback approach.

There are two major approaches for designing chargeback procedures:
- Fair value paid for services—In this approach, the function of the chargeback procedures is simply to charge users for the cost of the resources they use.
- Encourage and discourage the use of certain services—In this approach,

management uses chargeback procedures to influence user decisions about which services to use and when to use them. For example, management may want to discourage immediate online inquiry and encourage overnight inquiry. To achieve this, they can establish a much higher rate for immediate inquiry. Those who really need the service will still use it, but marginal users will be encouraged to take advantage of the lower rate for overnight inquiry.

CHARGEBACK OBJECTIVES

DP often represents a sizable investment of corporate resources and requires the same planning as that needed for other major investments. Planning includes setting objectives and determining the means for attaining these objectives. Chargeback procedures are one means of attaining management objectives in a DDP environment.

The DDP objectives that can be achieved with the help of chargeback procedures include:
- User accountability—Chargeback makes users accountable for their own actions through a series of charges that they must justify to management.
- Selecting among processing alternatives—Chargeback procedures assist users in decisions about alternate processing solutions.
- Balancing demand for services—The time frame in which services are requested can be affected by the charges made for those services. When charges are equal for all time periods, users will request services at the time most convenient for them. When charges vary for a service, depending on the time of day or week when this service is provided, users will think twice about requesting the service when charges are highest. By charging more for services during peak processing periods, management can give users an incentive to request services during off-peak hours, thus smoothing out the processing work loads.
- Orderly integration of new technology—By varying chargeback amounts over a period of time, management can gradually encourage the use of new resources. For example, the initial charges for DDP can be made very high to weed out all but the few users who really need distributed capability. This permits an orderly integration of DDP technology into the organization.

WHAT IS DIFFERENT ABOUT DISTRIBUTED SYSTEMS?

DP departments have been charging users for their services for at least 10 years. Many mainframe vendors provide utility programs to calculate chargeback amounts. For example, IBM offers Systems Management Facility (SMF) on their large mainframe equipment.

The obvious question then is, What is new about distributed systems that requires an organization to rethink existing chargeback procedures? If there are no differences, then existing chargeback procedures should be continued;

however, there *are* important differences between distributed and nondistributed systems that should affect chargeback procedures.

The word "distributed" is used so often that its meaning frequently becomes obscured. Organizations must determine whether there are real differences between their current DDP system and their previous method of operation.

The differences between distributed and nondistributed systems that require an organization to reassess chargeback procedures include:
- Absence of centralized control—In true distributed systems, there is little or no centralized control over the operation of the system. Each user can operate independently of all other users. Such systems must be coordinated; however, coordination usually lacks the authority found in most centralized systems.
- Capability to reject requests—Each workstation in a distributed system is autonomous and can opt to accept or reject requests from other workstations. Special procedures can be developed to store requests until they can be accepted or to cause users to search elsewhere for service.
- Users direct operations—Users schedule their own work, and a supply of work cannot be held for processing at slack times, as in centralized systems. In a distributed system, a work overload may occur at one point in time and be immediately followed by a slack period. There is no easy method of smoothing the work load because of the autonomy of the users.
- Resources are movable—Most processing resources in a distributed system can be "moved" when needed. One of the objectives of distributed systems is to be able to shift resources wherever they are needed. The cost of moving and storing the resources must be considered when developing a distributed chargeback algorithm.

The existence of one or more of these differences may necessitate rethinking of chargeback algorithms.

CHOOSING RESOURCES FOR CHARGEBACK

The following list of DDP resources is intended as a guide for use when considering which resources to include in a chargeback algorithm. It should be remembered that the overriding factors in determining chargeback procedures are simplicity and ease of use. Generalized charges therefore are often used (e.g., an organization may charge for CPU minutes rather than compile charges for the use of all individual equipment components). The following resource costs might be included in a chargeback algorithm:
- Online hardware—includes the cost for the computer and all peripheral equipment. The basis of the charge may be rental, lease, or depreciation costs. If the equipment is owned, maintenance charges should be included.

USER CHARGEBACK

- Offline hardware—Costs for all supportive equipment (e.g., bursters, slitters) are included here.
- Software—includes expenses incurred in connection with the rental, lease, or ownership of software packages. These charges may include software maintenance costs.
- Software developed in-house—includes costs for development staff and computer use. The cost for developing software in-house is usually charged directly at the time the software is developed.
- Communications facilities—includes the cost of communications lines and supporting equipment (e.g., communications controllers) needed to make the lines operational.
- Data base—includes the cost of establishing and maintaining data independently of the hardware and software needed for that data. Included here are charges for data base administration support personnel and facilities, operation of the data dictionary, and maintenance of data documentation support systems.
- Processing capabilities—includes costs for the units of work performed on distributed systems. This cost may be used in lieu of, or in addition to, hardware and software costs.
- Movement of resources—Pieces of hardware, software, personnel, data storage media, and data may all be moved from one user area to another. Charges include moving costs and the cost incurred because of the loss of resources during the move.
- Message rejections—Users can opt to accept or reject messages from another user. The rejection of messages results in a storage and inconvenience charge that may be charged either to the user rejecting the message or to the user requesting service.
- Support personnel—includes staff and facilities charges involved in coordinating the distributed system.
- Support hardware and software—includes the cost of any hardware or software needed to keep the system in operation.
- Priorities—Messages and jobs may carry different priorities, with higher charges assessed for higher-priority work.
- Direct administrative charges—includes charges that can be directly associated with distributed systems (e.g., charges for insurance, supplies, tapes, disk packs, ribbons, continuous forms, manuals).
- Indirect administrative expenses—includes administrative charges that are difficult to associate directly with distributed systems. These include costs for property taxes, heat, light, general training courses, mail services, and administrative support services (e.g., payroll).

Some or all of these charges may be included in the chargeback algorithms. The chargeback approach established can help determine which of the charges should be included. For example, if the organization wants to charge for fair value consumed, all of the above items should be included in the algorithm. If the main objective of the chargeback procedures is to discourage the use of a particular service, the rate charged need not be calculated using all of these detailed costs.

CHARGEBACK DATA COLLECTION METHODS

Before charges are allocated, accurate data on services used must be collected. The collection method can affect the reliability of the data—data collected manually is often less reliable than data collected automatically. Three methods are commonly used to collect chargeback information, including:

- Automated collection methods—Automated chargeback data is collected as a by-product of the work performed. For example, each message sent is counted for chargeback purposes. If the algorithm is simple, the automated method of data collection is usually the most effective and most economical.
- Financial accounting charges and allocations—Allocations are made to the distributed processing system, using information collected for financial accounting purposes. For example, if special printer forms are ordered, charges for the forms can be directed to the user ordering the forms. Personnel charges from the payroll system or cost system can be allocated directly to users, either as a direct charge or as an allocation percentage.
- Manual reports—This method requires that the staff record chargeback information on log sheets (i.e., programmers or computer operators must record the number of hours they work on a specific job). This is the least reliable collection method because it relies on the staff to record accurate information on a timely basis.

As with each aspect of the chargeback system, the data collection method will vary with the objectives set for the system. Only when clear objectives are set up can management choose a method that will produce data with the necessary reliability to meet those objectives. For example, a terminal operator usage log may suffice for a generalized chargeback algorithm designed to make users accountable for their activity; however, this method would not be reliable enough to enable management to charge for the specific DDP system components used.

Criteria for Measuring Usage

Management must decide which criteria will be implemented to measure resource usage. For example, should programmer effort be charged in hours, lines of coding, or some other unit of measurement? The unit of measure used to record resource use should also be the basis for user chargeback. Some common measures for resource utilization are listed in Table 6-1.

Recording methods for this data range from very complex to very simple. The more complex methods (e.g., IBM's Systems Management Facility) attempt to record and measure every resource utilized. SMF records each time a file is opened, each time a record is read or written into a file, each time a hardware device is used, and so on.

Not all chargeback algorithms are complex, however; some organizations use very simple chargeback algorithms, such as:

USER CHARGEBACK

Table 6-1. Resource Utilization Measures

Resource Measured	Unit of Measurement
Systems personnel	Hours of effort
Programmers	Lines of computer code
DDP coordinators	Hours of effort
Lead terminal	Total cost allocated among users as an overhead percentage of other charges
Communications lines	Actual line charges or number of transmissions
On-site resources	Total cost of on-site resources *or* Total cost of on-site resources less resources consumed by other users
System hardware resources	Percentage of total cost of resources consumed *or* Number of transactions processed
Special services	Actual cost of those services
General administrative charges	Total cost allocated among all users as an overhead percentage of their other charges
Priority service	A surcharge based on priority classification (the higher the priority classification, the higher the surcharge)
Message refused and stored awaiting acceptance	No charge *or* A storage charge if the message is held in queue
Unused resources	Usually included in the charge assessed for resources utilized
Direct administrative charges	Allocation based on total of all other charges
Data base	Amount of direct-access storage consumed *or* Number of transactions/data elements contained in the data base *or* Number of requests for data
Non-data-base files	Mounting and dismounting files *or* Size of file *or* Activity against file

- Single time charge—As with telephone system charges, a user is charged X dollars per minute when attached to the DDP system. A user can operate in an offline mode and not be charged; however, when the user is connected to the system, a standard charge begins to accumulate.
- Fixed percentage of cost—The costs for the entire system are totaled and divided among the users, based on a fixed percentage that may or may not be based on resources consumed.
- Size of user—Users may pay charges based upon some size factor (e.g., number of employees, sales volume).
- Resources allocated—When a user department joins a DDP system, it may be allocated a certain amount of resources (e.g., on-site hardware,

data storage capacity). Charges are made based on these allocated resources.

CALCULATING DDP CHARGEBACK COSTS

It is important to keep in mind the impact of chargeback procedures on the use of DDP facilities. Chargeback procedures should not be developed independently; rather, they should be developed hand in hand with other procedures for the distributed environment. The following paragraphs discuss how chargeback rates are established.

The cost of executing a unit of work in a distributed facility is not directly proportional to the amount of work performed. A large part of the cost of a DDP system will be incurred regardless of whether or not the facilities are used. These fixed costs cover the hardware, software, personnel, and administrative support involved in keeping the facilities available for use.

As the volume of work increases, the cost increases slowly. The cost line in Figure 6-1 starts at a fixed amount and increases slowly to reflect the additional charges incurred in doing more work on the system. The slowly increasing cost represents the variable costs (e.g., additional rental, staff, communications lines, supplies needed to process the increased work load). Some of these variable costs, however, (e.g., owned communications lines) will change very little because of an increased volume of work.

A chargeback rate must be determined that will exactly recoup all DDP costs. The point where the total amount charged to users equals costs is called the chargeback break-even point. If the chargeback rate is too high, the DDP system will make a "paper" profit for the organization; if it is too low, the DDP system will show a "paper" loss.

With a fair value approach, the ideal chargeback rate is the chargeback break-even point. This point is calculated using the following equation:

$$\text{Chargeback Rate per Unit of Work} = \frac{\text{Total DDP System Costs}}{\text{Estimated Units of Work at Break-Even Point}}$$

A simplified example of this technique can be developed using "messages processed" as the unit of work. Charges are based on the number of messages processed and do not depend on the type of processing needed for a message. If the cost to operate the DDP system is $250,000 per year, and 10,000 messages are processed per year, then the chargeout rate is $25 per message ($250,000 divided by 10,000 messages equals $25 per message).

If the number of units of work is overestimated, the chargeback amount will be too low and the system will not recoup costs. For example, if the rate of $25 per message is used but only 8,000 messages are processed, $50,000 will be lost and the DP department will fall within the DDP loss area illustrated in Figure 6-1. If, however, the number of units of work actually

USER CHARGEBACK

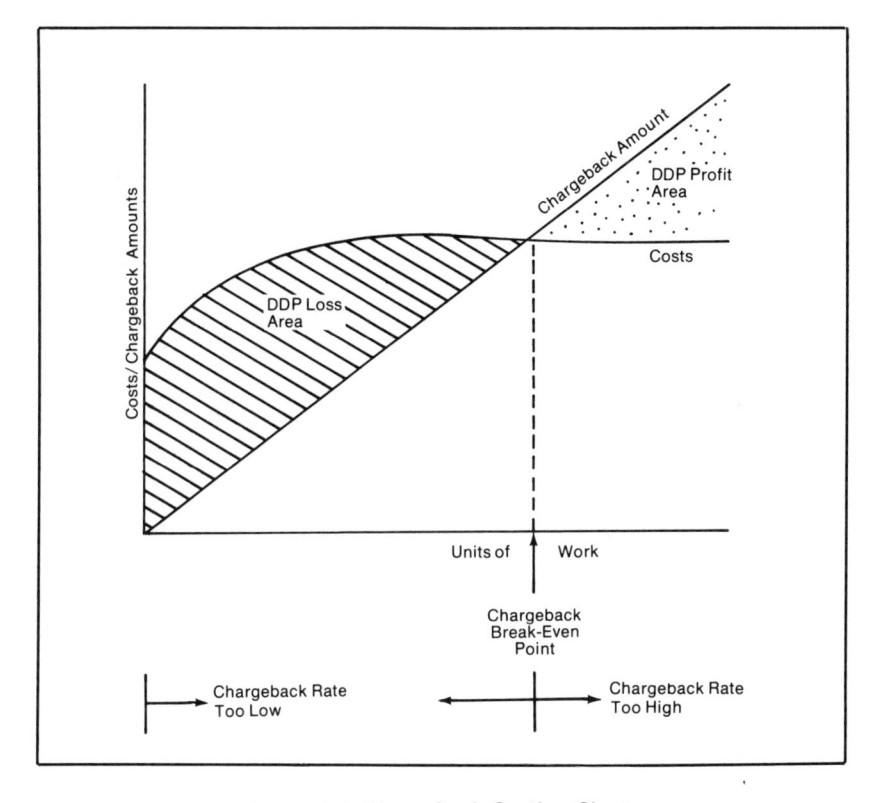

Figure 6-1. Chargeback Costing Chart

performed is underestimated, the DP department will fall within the DDP profit area shown in Figure 6-1.

To avoid a loss or profit position, many DP departments have adopted strategies such as:
- Adjusting the rate every three or six months to reflect changing conditions.
- Adjusting user charges at the end of each accounting period or year to reflect actual costs. Depending on whether the period results in a loss or a profit, the DP department will make an additional charge to a user or provide a billing adjustment for overcharging during the period.
- Transferring the profit or loss to the organization's overhead so that it can be billed to the departments together with all other administrative charges.

Costing algorithms can be as simple or as complex as necessary to achieve the desired objectives. For example, a very simple algorithm would be based on transactions or messages processed, number of CPU minutes used, and/or facilities installed in the user area. The more complex charging algorithms attempt to identify individual elements of cost attributable to each user.

CONTROLLING DDP SYSTEMS WITH CHARGEBACK PROCEDURES

As stated previously, it is important that chargeback procedures are developed as an integral part of DDP systems planning. If developed independently, chargeback procedures may have a negative impact on the accomplishment of planning objectives. In such cases users may hear two messages: one message (the plans) that tells them what management says it wants, and a louder message (the chargeback procedures) saying, This is what management really wants because this is how we will be held accountable for the use of DDP resources.

Chargeback procedures can be developed by top management or by DP management. DP management uses the procedures to direct users to employ resources in the manner they believe is most beneficial for the organization as a whole. Top management has other options for restricting and encouraging the use of certain resources. For example, top management is responsible for approving budgets. In the budgetary process, they can restrict or expand any user's capabilities. If they do not want a user to gain access to more DDP resources, they can prevent this by disapproving the budgetary request for those resources.

Management considerations that should be evaluated when developing chargeback procedures include:

- User control over facilities—DDP systems give users great control over resources. Charges can be developed to reflect the amount of control a user can exercise over those resources. For example, a user who demands exclusive use of resources during normal working hours can be charged more for those facilities than can another user who shares the resources with other users during normal working hours.
- User-owned resources—In some organizations users can buy and install their own computer facilities, which are then connected to a distributed system in a cooperative venture. In these instances the chargeback algorithm can either encourage or discourage users to buy their own hardware. When the resources are centrally owned, management usually has more control over what type of equipment is used.
- Single-user facilities—If a special piece of hardware or software is needed for a single user, that user should be charged the entire cost for these facilities. A prohibitive cost for such services will encourage users to use standard facilities.
- Facilities for limited numbers of users—If facilities are obtained for a limited number of users, only the involved users should be charged for the use of these facilities. For example, if a distributed system has 20 users, and a software package is obtained for three of those users, the cost of that software package should be allocated only among the three users requesting it.
- Lead terminal charges—Usually one terminal is designated as the lead terminal, or lead node, in the system. Since many of the functions

performed on this lead terminal benefit all users, the charges for these functions should be allocated among all users.

CONCLUSION

Chargeback procedures are an effective method for controlling DDP systems. The main advantage of a DDP system is that each user has increased control over his own processing needs; however, true DDP systems lack strong central control. Chargeback procedures can increase control over user consumption of DDP resources. Because of the lack of central control in DDP systems, top management should be involved in developing chargeback procedures. If DDP users attempt to develop their own procedures, they might have difficulty reaching an agreement on procedures that restrict their use of the system. Top management must be involved if they want to use chargeback procedures for control purposes other than allocating charges for resources used.

The following steps are recommended for developing an effective chargeback procedure in a DDP system:
- Establish the objectives the organization hopes to achieve by implementing and operating the distributed system.
- Determine which of the objectives can be aided by the implementation of a user chargeback system.
- Design chargeback procedures that will aid in achieving the objectives.
- Monitor the use of distributed facilities to determine whether or not the objectives established by management are being achieved. If the objectives are being achieved, the chargeback procedures are probably effective.
- If management objectives for the DDP system are not being achieved, the chargeback procedures should be adjusted to influence users to choose the options that coincide with management objectives.

7 Establishing Standards for Distributed Processing

by Grayce M. Booth

INTRODUCTION

Any organization considering or planning a DDP system should also think about establishing standards to ensure maximum efficiency and flexibility for the system and staff. Concern for standardization is often appropriate, even when an organization operates multiple, independent, decentralized computer systems rather than an integrated DDP network. The increasing need to exchange data among systems often leads organizations to link previously freestanding systems.

OBJECTIVES OF STANDARDIZATION

There are four major objectives involved in setting internal DDP standards. Three of these objectives apply to all organizations involved in DDP; the fourth applies only in specific cases. The four objectives of standardization are:
- Compatibility of system components
- Improved productivity in applications development
- Simplified procedures for terminal users
- Program transferability

Compatibility of System Components. This is the most basic reason for standardization. Very often, computing equipment is procured at different times, or by different groups, or for different applications. This often leaves the organization with a variety of equipment types that cannot exchange data or be coordinated in a distributed system.

This may be perfectly acceptable if data exchange is not needed (i.e., if the equipment will continue to be used in a decentralized mode of operation); however, many applications implemented independently are later found to require interconnection. The need for data exchange continues to grow as organizations become more complex. Office automation systems will also increase the need for linking systems within an organization, as WP and electronic mail are gradually integrated with traditional DP operations.

Each of these factors indicates a need for interconnection standards to be applied in all equipment procurements. This is much more efficient than attempting to link incompatible elements at a later date.

Improved Productivity in Applications Development. If computing equipment is acquired without controls, the result may be a collection of different devices with different programming languages, different data base management systems, and so on. Each set of characteristics requires additional programmer training and may limit the interchangeability of programmers in different groups.

This does not mean that all equipment must be identical; that would unnecessarily restrict the organization's flexibility. It is usually advantageous, however, to ensure that a specific set of software features—especially programming languages—is available on all equipment used.

Simplified Procedures for Terminal Users. This is very important in DDP or in any online system. If a terminal user accesses several application systems, it is important that these systems provide common user interfaces and that documentation on how to use the terminal is consistent for all applications.

In a distributed system, one terminal user can access different components of the system (e.g., a local satellite processor and a central host processor) at different times. Inadequate standards can lead to differences in documentation and procedures that confuse terminal users and reduce their productivity.

Program Transferability. The ability to transfer programs among distributed sites is, in some cases, another reason for having standards. For example, if an application is implemented on a central host computer and later distributed to satellite processors at various point-of-transaction locations, it is valuable to be able to move the application programs from the host to the satellites without major changes.

Programs can rarely be moved from one computer to another in object form without any change. With appropriate standards, however, it may be possible to move the programs in source form simply by recompiling on the new processing system.

CATEGORIES OF DISTRIBUTED SYSTEMS

When considering the need for DDP standards, it is essential to determine which of the following categories the planned DDP system fits. Standardization requirements vary for each type of system.

Loosely Coupled DDP Systems. These systems consist of free-standing clusters of activities linked only for data exchange. An example of this type of distributed system is shown in Figure 7-1.

In this example the system consists of two parts. One part handles inventory control and orders from sales offices, and the other handles the manufac-

ESTABLISHING STANDARDS

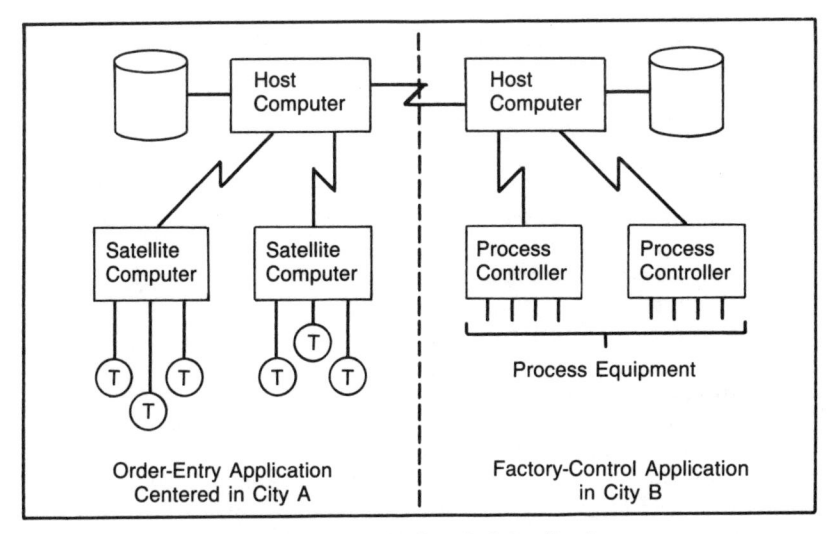

Figure 7-1. Loosely Coupled Applications

turing process in the firm's factory. Each half of the system can operate semi-independently; however, they are related. Decreased inventory caused by sales can trigger a need for factory production; conversely, factory output must also be reflected in inventory. The interconnection between the applications allows these essential operations to occur.

In this type of system, the different applications are often implemented by separate application development groups. Without appropriate standards, interconnection and data exchange can be difficult. In addition to interconnection, logical compatibility is required to ensure that the data exchanged can be understood. For example, the order-entry application might describe stocked items in terms of marketing identifiers, while the factory-control application might use internal part numbers. Thus, some method of cross-referencing would be required for one or both of the applications.

Highly Integrated DDP Systems. A highly integrated DDP system usually requires less attention to standards because the entire system implementation is usually carried out by one development group. A distributed system for online branch banking, for example, may include multiple computing facilities at branch locations, but these facilities must all work together very closely. As a result, a centralized development approach is often used. The standardization found in most centralized DP organizations is generally adequate to handle this situation.

It is important to remember, however, that highly integrated DDP systems may evolve over time into more loosely coupled arrangements. The branch banking system, for example, might be linked to the bank's system for processing credit card business or, in the case of a European bank, to a system for handling stock accounts. In addition, many systems of this type will gradually be loosely coupled with electronic mail facilities. Looking ahead to these possibilities makes attention to standards appropriate even in highly integrated DDP systems.

AREAS FOR STANDARDIZATION

When an organization decides to define internal standards for DDP, seven areas of standardization should be considered. In most cases it is necessary to set standards for each area. The seven areas are:
- Guidelines for functional centralization and/or distribution
- Compatibility standards
- Data base standards
- Application development standards
- Procedures for application and data base change
- Integrity, security, privacy, and accountability standards
- Documentation standards

Each of these areas is discussed in depth in the following paragraphs to enable planners to determine whether a particular class of standards is required in their organization.

Guidelines for Functional Centralization and/or Distribution

It is important to establish guidelines concerning which types of functions or applications should be centralized and which should be distributed. If guidelines are not established, each development group will make these decisions independently, and inefficient designs may result. Guidelines, rather than standards, are suggested here because it is very difficult to foresee all conditions that must be considered when deciding whether to centralize or distribute.

Technical Factors. Technical issues must be considered when establishing these guidelines. For example, certain functions, such as data entry and typical WP, are often most cost-effective when performed on a mini- or micro-based processor. These functions are therefore good candidates for distribution. On the other hand, functions such as management of a large data base or control of archival storage are usually more cost-effective on a large computer and are therefore good candidates for centralization.

Managerial Control. Another factor in establishing these guidelines is managerial control. Functions that are important to higher levels of management often require tight control and increased security measures. It is usually best to centralize such functions. Functions that are primarily of local interest and are locally controlled should usually be distributed.

Privacy and Security. In some systems, privacy or security protection must also be considered. Data or programs that require a high level of protection (for industrial or governmental security reasons or to protect personal privacy) usually should be centralized. Data and programs that are publicly accessible and do not require tight protection can be distributed.

ESTABLISHING STANDARDS

Cost Considerations. Finally, various cost factors enter into the establishment of these guidelines. For example, equipment procured for use in remote locations usually must be able to operate in an open office environment, without attention from DP operations personnel, because a special environment and trained, dedicated operations personnel are often economically infeasible at distributed sites. The guidelines established by the organization should prevent acquisition of DDP equipment that cannot be used in such an office environment.

Compatibility Standards

Equipment procured by different groups or at different times may be difficult to coordinate in a distributed system. In the future, however, more of the DP and office automation equipment operated by any organization will be linked. Compatibility standards that must be observed in all equipment procurements will facilitate this linking.

The most important level of compatibility is in network or interconnection protocols. Requiring that all equipment support a specific set of protocols ensures the ability to interconnect the equipment as needed. Network protocols include many levels, the first of which is basic physical connection. Many types of computer and terminal equipment support the EIA (Electronic Industries Association) RS-232C interface, which allows connection to standard modems and therefore to telephone networks. (A more complex new interface, RS-449, has recently been defined by the EIA and will gradually be phased into use in place of RS-232C.)

Higher-level network protocols control the transfer of data and the decoding of its meaning. Some protocols of this type include teleprinter, Binary Synchronous Communications (BSC), Synchronous Data Link Control (SDLC), and High-Level Data Link Control (HDLC). Any one of these protocols—most of which have several forms and options—can provide data exchange between components.

The trend toward using value-added networks (VANs) in the United States and public data networks (PDNs) in other countries is leading to widespread support of the CCITT (Consultative Committee for International Telephone and Telegraphy) X.25 recommendation for standard interconnection. Although X.25 was formulated for connecting computer and terminal equipment to public data networks, it is also possible to build an entirely private network using X.25.

Interconnection standards are complex and should be studied in considerable detail. Lack of compatibility standards in this area can lead to anarchy in DDP.

Compatibility standards are also needed for programming languages and data base management system (DBMS) software. These must define the languages and DBMS required on each type of equipment procured. For standard business DP systems, COBOL is by far the most popular and widely used language. Use of COBOL for all business programming minimizes the amount of programmer training or retraining needed and helps to achieve program transferability. Some organizations find that RPG is suitable for programming simpler business applications. RPG is not widely used on large computers; however, on small or medium-scale computers it can improve programmer productivity.

Standards for programming languages should be as specific as possible. COBOL, for example, is defined in standards issued by the American National Standards Institute (ANSI). Within the ANSI COBOL language definition, however, are a number of optional features and levels of support. This results in wide disparity between a COBOL compiler that implements the lowest-possible ANSI-standard level and one that implements the entire standard, including all options (and possibly including nonstandard extensions). Both can legitimately be called ANSI COBOL. When setting standards, features and options must be specified. If feasible, acceptable subsets may also be defined.

For applications that require a data base, DBMS compatibility standards must also be developed. The only industry standard in this area defines what are often called CODASYL data bases because the Conference on Data Systems Languages (CODASYL) originated the methods for describing and accessing data bases with complex structures. Programming methods for accessing these data bases are included (as an option) in the COBOL language definition. DBMS standards must at least define common procedures for programmers accessing the data bases; in many cases this is most easily achieved by standardizing the type of DBMS software used.

Of course, many DDP components do not support a complex data base. Examples include word processors, terminal controllers, concentrators, and similar devices. Many of these small, specialized components are not programmed to support application processing. For this reason, compatibility standards must precisely state which requirements apply to each type of equipment.

Data Base Standards

An online or DDP system usually includes one or more data bases (either centralized or distributed). These data bases are valuable assets of the organization; it is important to protect them. Standards for the establishment and control of data bases will aid in providing this protection.

Administrative management of a data base is usually the responsibility of a data base administrator (DBA) or a DBA staff. The DBA staff performs three functions:
- Ensures that each data base is designed and developed in accordance with appropriate standards
- Controls changes in the structure or content of the data base when such changes are needed
- Monitors data base use to detect current or potential problems

ESTABLISHING STANDARDS 91

Because the concept of data base control by a DBA staff is widely accepted, the major requirement in this area is to define standards that cover the interaction of multiple DBA staffs in a loosely coupled DDP system or a decentralized system.

For the DDP system described in Figure 7-1, standards must define how data exchange occurs between the order-entry-system data base and the factory-control-system data base. If common data elements are stored in duplicate in both data bases, guidelines are needed to ensure compatibility. Data synchronization procedures must also be defined, ensuring that changes in data content that affect both data bases are reflected appropriately in both. Finally, because any change in the data structure of either data base may affect the other, such changes must be coordinated.

These problems are more easily managed in a tightly coupled DDP application with a single DBA staff. Loosely coupled systems, however, usually have more than one DBA staff. Coordination among the staffs can be improved by a set of standard procedures and methods for ensuring data base compatibility and synchronization. This is also true in decentralized systems if there is a current or potential relationship among the data bases on freestanding systems.

Application Development Standards

Standards for developing DDP applications are closely related to compatibility standards for equipment acquisition. Although they are aimed at different groups, these two sets of standards should be developed together.

Application development standards must define which programming languages are to be used for each type of DDP application and which DBMS software is to be used, especially if the computer(s) used offer more than one choice.

If it is desirable to transfer some application programs among different computer equipment—either periodically or dynamically (during system operation)—it may be necessary to define language subsets (and perhaps DBMS subsets) for these applications. Using a subset of a language such as COBOL, rather than the complete language, increases the probability that programs will be transferable between two or more types of computers.

These standards must also define the user interface design for online applications. A consistent approach to the design of user interfaces minimizes user confusion. These standards must be closely coordinated with the standards for user documentation because much of the documentation is online and integrated into the application programs.

When defining application development standards, it is also important to specify the types of applications to which these standards apply. Standards must apply to all continuing production applications; they need not apply to one-time reports, test programs, and similar applications.

Procedures for Application and Data Base Changes

Most DP organizations have defined procedures for initiating changes to existing applications or for changing the structure or content of an existing data base. In DDP, standards must ensure that changes affecting multiple components or locations in the system are made consistently in all affected areas. This concern is especially important in loosely coupled distributed systems.

The system in Figure 7-1 serves as an example again. A change in the manufacturing process might necessitate specification of one of two possible options for each product of a particular type. This would require a corresponding change in order-entry procedures and applications to include the option in all new orders. An option field might have to be added to the manufacturing in-process data base records and to the order and inventory data base records. These changes must be coordinated in manufacturing and order entry.

Integrity, Security, Privacy, and Accountability Standards

The methods for providing appropriate levels of integrity, security, privacy, and accountability must also be standardized in a DDP or decentralized system. Integrity protection ensures the accuracy of the data being processed and stored and provides the ability to recover from error and failure situations. Data bases at distributed sites may contain the only copy of specific business information, and integrity protection is required to ensure that this data is not lost or damaged through system error or failure.

Security and privacy controls are concerned with protecting the system and stored data from theft, damage, or disclosure (intentional or accidental). Both distributed and decentralized systems require special attention to security and privacy controls; computer resources (and sometimes data bases) are often placed at locations that lack the physical protection of central computer sites.

Accountability standards ensure the auditability of the system and the ability to establish system costs and allocate them fairly among users (if cost allocation is used).

The areas of integrity, security, privacy, and accountability are all technically complex, and remote-site personnel implementing a decentralized system or a node in a loosely coupled DDP system may be unfamiliar with current techniques. Standards and guidelines established by an expert DP and auditing staff are essential for successful implementations.

Documentation Standards

Comprehensive documentation standards are an important consideration in DDP. Special attention should be given to standards for documentation for terminal users. As mentioned previously, one terminal user may access multiple applications residing in multiple computers. The user must see a single, consistent interface, regardless of the complexity of the supporting system.

User documentation standards should apply to written manuals and other forms of hard-copy documentation, as well as to the online documentation provided at the terminal. An increasing number of user interfaces are almost completely tutorial, and written user documentation may not be provided.

Program Documentation. Standards are also required for program documentation. These standards often exist in centralized DP organizations; however, they are sometimes not strictly enforced. DDP systems are often more complex than are centralized systems and usually change more frequently; thus, standard program documentation is of great importance. Application developers in a DDP system may have to analyze many parts of a large system to determine the effect of proposed program changes. This analysis can only be accomplished efficiently if documentation is complete and standardized.

Operational Documentation. Documentation to be used by operations personnel (e.g., console operators) must also be standardized. This does not necessarily mean that only one type of operational documentation is required. Many DDP systems have two sets of operations procedures—and two corresponding types of documentation.

The first set of procedures is used at the typical central or host DP site, with trained console operators, tape and disk librarians, and so on. The documentation used at such sites is similar to that used in centralized systems. The procedures manual is the primary form of documentation.

The second type of operational procedure applies to remote locations, where there are often no trained DP personnel. Someone at these locations must be able to start DDP equipment (e.g., satellite processors, terminal controllers). Procedures must be available for such tasks as loading and removing paper from the printer, replacing printer ribbons or cartridges, exchanging disk packs or cartridges, and handling equipment malfunctions.

Although these are operational procedures, the standards for this documentation should be similar to those established for terminal user documentation. In fact, the local equipment will often be operated by terminal users. Documentation that is easy to understand and use is crucial to smooth operation. As much of this documentation as possible should be online and tutorial; of course, instructions on handling system outages must be maintained in hard-copy form.

STANDARDIZATION METHODS

The preceding section describes the areas in which each organization should define DDP-related standards. Before defining appropriate standards, however, each organization must answer these questions:
- Who will establish the standards?
- Who will enforce them and how?

There is no point in spending the time and effort necessary to establish a good set of standards if they will not be observed. Management involvement and support are important to ensure that the standards will meet the needs of the organization.

Establishing Standards

Establishing DDP guidelines and standards is a complex process involving decisions on organization-wide managerial policy and attention to many technical details. Interconnection protocol standards, for example, involve quite complex technical issues. At the same time, technical planners may choose interconnection standards (either intentionally or through oversight) that can be met only by one vendor's equipment. This may be inconsistent with management objectives. To prevent such problems, the group or groups who define standards should possess both technical expertise and managerial background. This balance can be achieved in several ways.

A medium-sized organization might establish a technical standards committee responsible for defining all necessary DDP standards. A separate review and approval committee might be authorized to approve all new standards and any modifications to existing standards. This group would be less technically oriented but would be responsible for ensuring that the standards support management goals and objectives.

A very large organization might choose to establish multiple specialized technical committees. One committee might handle language compatibility and usage standards, another might handle documentation standards, and so on. The technical committees might submit proposed standards to a single review and approval group.

In a small organization, a single standards group might include both technical and management representatives. This group would be responsible for both defining and approving standards.

Regardless of the organization's size, the users (or prospective users) of the DDP system should participate in the definition of standards. Standards for the development of user interfaces and user documentation must take into account the specific users and their needs. Involving user representatives in the development process will help ensure appropriate standards and will also help establish good relationships with the users—an important factor in the success of any system.

Enforcing Standards

Once standards have been established, they must be enforced. Procedures must be set up to ensure that each equipment procurement is reviewed for compliance with the guidelines and standards. Procedures are also required for reviewing new or changed programs and documentation to ensure that the appropriate standards are observed.

Equipment procurements and overall DDP plans should be reviewed by both management representatives and technical personnel. Programs and documentation require technical review, and user documentation must also be

ESTABLISHING STANDARDS

reviewed by user representatives. (As discussed previously, operational documentation for remote sites usually falls into the same category as user documentation.)

Organizational Considerations

When defining and enforcing DDP standards, the particular organization's structure and style must be considered. Because of the complexity of this topic, it is impossible to provide an in-depth discussion that covers all possible types of organizations; however, some major issues can be identified.

Representation on Standards Committees. In an organization with multiple DP installations, all affected groups should be represented on the committees that delimit technical standards. If this is not done, groups not represented on the committees may resist standardization. In a large organization, however, full representation may lead to the formation of large, unwieldy committees, who have difficulty making decisions. In such cases a trade-off must be made to ensure adequate representation without excessive committee size.

The same rules apply to representation for system users. User involvement is crucial; however, it can lead to adversary situations and impasses in decision making unless methods are devised for breaking deadlocks. In addition, it may be appropriate to include different user representatives on technical committees at different times, depending on which groups are most affected by specific standards.

In a decentralized system in which some applications are implemented locally without a DP staff, local implementors/users must be involved in the standardization process. Care is necessary in such situations to avoid the hostility that can easily arise between local groups and a central DP organization.

Management involvement and the level of the organization at which standards are approved and enforced are also complex issues. As information systems move from the traditional batch DP shop and into direct support of operations, it becomes essential for higher-level management—especially line management—to be represented in the decision-making process.

The specific method of representation depends mainly on the management style of the organization. With a centralized management structure, management representation can come from the central staff. In an organization with decentralized management, wider representation is required to ensure adequate input on the requirements of different groups.

Appropriate Levels of Standardization. When developing a standardization program, the two extremes of paying too little attention to standards versus overstandardization must be avoided. In many organizations, establishing and enforcing standards is considered a spare-time activity. Often the people most technically qualified to define standards are already heavily committed to other tasks and are asked to spend time "as available" on standards committee work. Under these circumstances adequate time is seldom available. If management wants effective standards, they must realistically assess the need for standards and provide the necessary funding and support. Standards are often a prudent investment that provides a valuable payoff by preventing unnecessary system modifications and makeshift solutions.

It is important, however, not to overdo standardization. Many organizations perform a variety of rather loosely related activities. In many cases a minimal set of interconnection guidelines may be all that is required because most DP activities are semiautonomous and will remain decentralized. As mentioned previously, it may also be appropriate to define certain types of DP procurements and developments that are automatically exempt from standards (e.g., lab work in a university or one-time reporting programs in a business DP organization).

Information processing attracts many innovative people who can develop new solutions to processing problems. Standardization must avoid stifling this creativity. On the other hand, sufficient control is required to prevent innovation for its own sake, which can lead to overly complex, incompatible system solutions. An appropriate balance between standardization and freedom to innovate must be the goal of each organization involved in DDP.

CONCLUSION

Many organizations begin to distribute DP systems on an application-by-application basis, without an overall set of guidelines and standards. In other cases, different groups within an organization may acquire low-cost equipment for local, decentralized data or text processing, without considering the possibility of interconnecting these systems in the future.

Long-range trends make it clear that most equipment used for typical DP, office automation, factory automation, and so on will eventually be linked with other equipment operated by the same organization. Management decisions and support are required to ensure that appropriate standards are established and enforced so that the transition to DDP will be as smooth as possible.

8 Designing an Integrated Communications Network

by José A. Trinidad

INTRODUCTION

Any organization operating a distributed processing network is confronted with the problems of data communications. If that network connects many computing facilities and covers geographically dispersed locations, communications costs can be a major problem for management. While more and more organizations are developing distributed data networks, technological advances such as competitively priced satellite links, light beam links, and all-digital transmission are on the communications horizon. These developments will make integrated communications networks (transmitting data, voice, fax, and video on common broadband links) a cost-effective solution to communications problems. To take advantage of these developments, networks developed today must be designed with tomorrow's goals in mind, and DDP planners must take a step back from their immediate data communications needs to get a broader view of network design issues.

This chapter provides a framework for designing a network that will be effective today as well as adaptable to the expected changes in communications technology.

STRATEGY FOR THE DESIGN PROCESS

Network design should be a sensible, step-by-step process, avoiding the ad hoc, reactive mode of design that is often used today. The rapid changes and immaturity of communications technology make the problem more difficult; however, there is enough evidence concerning which network trends will continue in the future to enable planners to follow a systematic design procedure. From these dominant communications trends, a sound set of assumptions can be defined and used to support the design process. With this basis, planners should address the pivotal areas involved in any network design and then establish a realistic methodology for implementing a network with today's resources but with tomorrow's goals in mind.

Dominant Communications Trends

The late 1970s was a time of important development in communications technology. Although this technology is still in the formative stages, several definite trends can be expected to continue. Three major trends are those toward digital transmission, much greater transmission capacities, and the integration of voice, data, and other transmission forms into one common transmission link.

In addition, the communications market has divided into three areas: long distance (LD), local area (LA), and premise loop (PL). Because of the different applications of technology in each area and the effect of government actions regarding communications, different vendors and product offerings are involved in each area.

The LD area has been opened to competition through the government's deregulatory actions. Satellite, microwave, and terrestrial links have increased the marketing opportunities for the many vendors who have entered the long-distance market. As a result, LD rates dropped dramatically throughout the 1970s, and competition will maintain this trend in the future.

LA rates, however, have escalated because competing with AT&T in the local business and residential areas requires huge capital investments. Although government regulation in this area has also been relaxed, any meaningful competition from such sources as microwave carriers is unlikely in the near future.

PL or office networks are not regulated at all; however, the technology in this area is embryonic. Nonetheless, PL networks will be a major concern in the 1980s and 1990s because the electronic office requires networking to connect the computers, data controllers, PBXs, and various types of automated equipment.

Assumptions

Because these communications trends are firmly established, the design process can be safely based on the following assumptions:
- The network should be designed to prepare for the ultimate integration of all transmission forms (voice, data, video, and image) into common digital transmission links.
- The network design should prepare to take advantage of large-capacity transmission links.
- The network should be designed in terms of the three market areas (LD, LA, and PL).

These assumptions also help to define the scope of the network design process, which is concerned only with network transfer functions (i.e., the means of transporting a unit of information from point A to point B).

Network transfer functions include transmission, switching, and network management. They do not include value-added functions such as protocol conversion or message storage and formatting, which belong to another level of network design more dependent on the transmission form itself (e.g., voice, data). Limiting the scope of the design to this level moves the network design process beyond the individual concerns of each transmission form and facilitates a comprehensive approach in which voice and data (and other

DESIGNING AN INTEGRATED NETWORK 99

transmission forms) are treated as common elements. This approach is necessary to prepare for the eventual integration of all transmission forms.

DESIGN FACTORS

These basic assumptions define the scope and level of the design process. The next logical step in this process is to determine the major factors that must be included in the design. There are five major factors in the design of an integrated communications network:
- Transmission forms
- Traffic
- Business requirements
- Operational requirements
- Network management

Transmission Forms

All transmission forms will have a common digital format by the end of the decade. In fact, most LD transmissions are currently digital, traveling at the same speeds and subject to the same hazards. What are the differences, then, among data, voice, and the other transmission forms? The only differences are found at the terminal end, in the mode of use of the information by the network's end elements. Computers can use the information from a transmission line 1,000 times faster than can humans. Image transmission poses different problems because humans require at least one megabit of information per second to be able to discern a visual image, and this image should preferably be continuous. Thus, before designing a network and laying down cables, planners should understand the absorption rates at the terminal ends, whether human, electronic, or electromechanical. Table 8-1 lists absorption rates for voice, data, and video. The different terminal absorption rates enable integrating the various transmission forms into one digital transmission (e.g., data can be transmitted during the pauses in digitized voice transmission).

Traffic

Traffic is the amount of information moving in and out of a facility (whether an office, a trunk, or an I/O device). Traffic has two dimensions, volume and direction, which must be measured to understand the manner in which a business uses each information form. Traffic profiles provide a basic picture of the organization's information flow patterns. Traffic is dependent on business needs, but it also reflects the organization's particular style—the human element that must be accounted for in the planning process.

Traffic must also be examined in terms of current and projected levels. Fortunately, traffic is easily measured, and numerous models have been developed to aid in analyzing traffic data and optimizing the topology of a voice or data network. By adding projections developed through simulation techniques, an analytical model of future traffic patterns can be obtained. Such a

Table 8-1. Absorption Rates of Human Sensory Organs and Electronic Terminals

	Bits per Second
Reading	400
Recognizable telephone speech	10K
Speech	20K
PCM telephone speech	56K
Hearing	200K
High-speed printer	500K
Minimal visual image	1M
Disk drive transfer rate	12M
Visual image (complete and continuous)	100M

model is "nice to have," although it may be unnecessary. Planners should keep in mind that traffic measurements are only one step in the design process and should not be considered an invariable factor. Traffic patterns can be altered through changes in other major design factors. For the network to be successful, all five major design factors must be balanced.

Business Requirements

Business requirements translate into network requirements (e.g., capacity, effectiveness, network accessibility, functions supported, convenience, and cost-effectiveness). They also influence the selection of network nodes, the degree of node clustering, and network organization (i.e., whether the network should be centralized, hierarchical, or linear). While traffic analysis quantifies network use, analysis of business requirements qualifies and projects future trends for that use.

Operational Requirements

The issues involved in operating the network must be dealt with as part of the design. These issues include:
- Is redundancy necessary?
- What are the reliability criteria for the network?
- How much security is needed?
- How easily can the network be changed?
- How easily can network performance be maintained?

Tolerances for network reliability, security, flexibility, and maintenance must be defined early in the design process.

Network Management

Finally, the whole purpose of establishing an integrated communications network is to provide services that will enhance the business. The functions of the network and the strategies for managing these functions are the final major factors in network design. Management issues that must be addressed include:
- Monitoring and measurement of network services
- Control

DESIGNING AN INTEGRATED NETWORK

- Billing for services
- Vendor and customer interfaces
- Planning

The five major factors in the design process are summarized in Table 8-2.

Table 8-2. Major Design Factors

Transmission Forms
  Voice
  Data
  Video
  Image

Traffic
  Volume
  Direction
  Current and projected levels

Business Requirements
  Location of network nodes
  Degree of node clustering
  Network organization (centralized, hierarchical, or linear)
  Expected growth (traffic projections)

Operational Considerations
  Reliability
  Security
  Flexibility
  Maintenance

Management Issues
  Measurement/monitoring
  Control
  Billing
  Vendor interface
  Customer interface
  Planning

DESIGNING THE THREE NETWORK AREAS

Regardless of the overall requirements of the business for centralization or dispersion of resources, a hierarchical network architecture that proceeds from PL to LA to LD is effective. The basic strategy is to link the PL sites in each metropolitan area or business center and then link the resulting LA networks into a global LD network. This hierarchical strategy (represented in Figure 8-1) allows great flexibility and provides an orderly framework for network design based on the market subdivisions. In addition, this strategy is designed to continuously merge traffic into wider transmission links to achieve the economies of scale their great capacity provides.

Based on this strategy, the design process moves through the following stages:
- Data collection
- PL network design (for each transmission form)
- LA network design (for each transmission form)
- LD network design (for each transmission form)

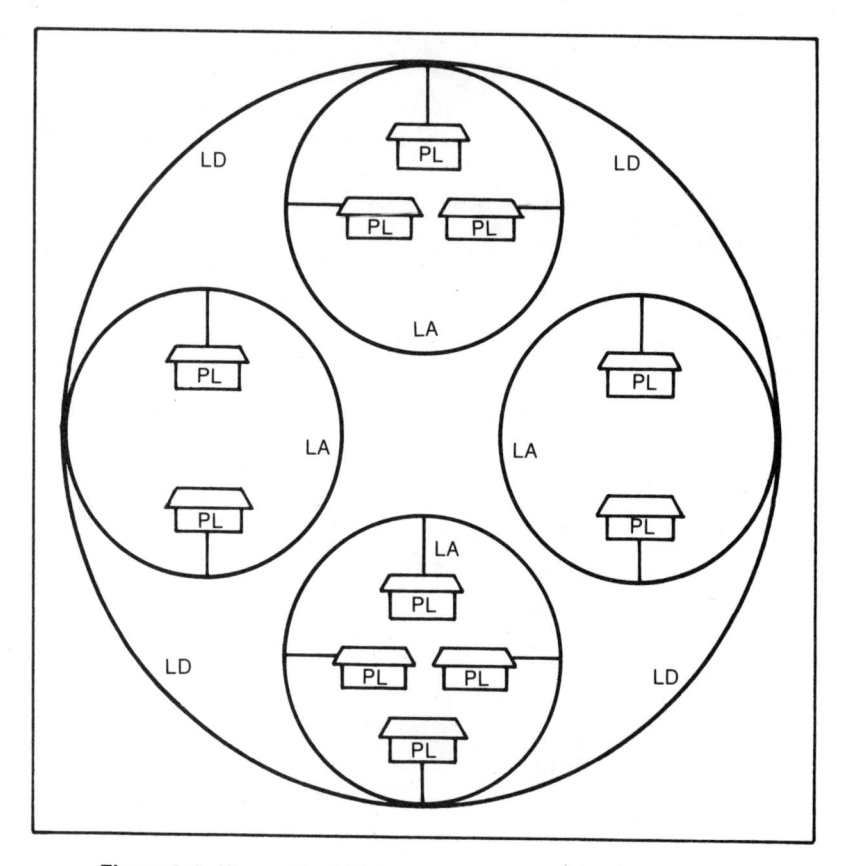

Figure 8-1. Hierarchical Linkup of PL, LA, and LD Networks

Each of the three network design stages includes four steps:
1. Analyze current traffic patterns for each transmission form.
2. Superimpose projected growth and management plans for each transmission form.
3. Compare the resulting voice and data networks, and analyze the possibilities for integration.
4. Optimize the resulting network.

The data for step 1 comes from the data collection process and includes traffic data and an inventory of current resources. The data for step 2 comes from the definitions established earlier for business, operations, and management requirements. Step 3 requires the analysis of voice and data requirements on a link-by-link basis to determine the possibility of integration. Step 4 is carried out using automated models, pencil and paper logic, or both.

Data Collection

Information about existing network resources in a large business is often surprisingly incomplete. This information is essential to the design process

DESIGNING AN INTEGRATED NETWORK

because once the major top-down strategies have been established, the design must efficiently integrate the current resources (representing a substantial capital investment) into the strategies for network development. An inventory of current facilities is a necessity for effective design. This inventory should also contain sufficient data about the cost of existing facilities to be used as a reference when analyzing future costs and savings. The inventory should cover hardware and link facilities. Included in the hardware category are computers, modems, controllers, concentrators, PBXs, telephone stations, data terminals, fax, telex, and so on. Link facilities include WATS, tie lines, FX lines, and satellite links. Traffic data should provide a location-by-location profile of communications traffic flow, including volume and destination.

This is by no means an easy task, and it must be planned well in advance. A system will be needed to keep the data updated after the initial data gathering because the design process is never concluded, and the fine tuning and management of the network require that the inventory be updated at least once a year.

Traffic information can be difficult to obtain unless adequate monitoring devices are used. Sophisticated data controllers and concentrators maintain this information as part of their normal operation. The carrier can also help with traffic data gathering. (Unfortunately, the data provided by carriers is seldom complete or timely.) For voice transmissions, traffic data collection is made more difficult by the fact that voice switches only entered the electronic age during the past decade. Because voice transmissions are slower and more tolerant than data transmissions, pressure has not been exerted on manufacturers to incorporate traffic-measuring functions into voice switches. Such functions are currently available—but at a significant cost.

The format of the traffic data should vary with the intended purpose. If the data will be fed into an automated simulation or optimization program, the requirements will be different from those for manual analysis. In either case, the data should be listed by transmissions link (trunk, microwave, or satellite), by time of day, and by day of the week. Some organizations may profit from collecting data over several months to establish long-term traffic patterns; however, this may be too expensive and time-consuming for an initial design. Intuition and paper and pencil can produce amazing results. Regardless of the follow-up, the traffic data is essential because it establishes quantitative levels for the traffic in and out of an office or switch.

PL Networks and the Problems of Integration

The design of premise networks or premise loops is only in the formative stage; however, this area will be the focus of much attention in the 1980s. Few of the available offerings even approach the problems of a premise loop facility. One such attempt is Xerox's ETHERNET, a passive, packetized data network. IBM's 8100 also uses the premise loop concept, but no existing global offering can integrate intraoffice transmissions into one network. Intraoffice transmission needs great improvement; indeed, integration of transmission forms depends on the development of systems that are designed to support PL networks.

When determining the premise location's place in the entire network, traffic patterns inside the premise are disregarded, and the design process concentrates on the transmissions moving out of or into the premise network.

Network Gates. The point where the PL network interfaces with the larger networks can be thought of as a gate, as shown in Figure 8-2. Currently, it is common to have as many gates as there are transmission forms (i.e., one for voice [PBX], one for data [controllers, concentrators], one for fax, and one for Telex); this arrangement is depicted in Figure 8-3. Although the slow-speed transmission forms (Telex, fax) can be sent over voice transmission links without trouble, the gates to those links are contained in the device performing the special Telex or fax functions. Currently, this is the simplest way to perform this function. The drawback of this method is that these messages are transmitted at the applicable voice rate, and the organization cannot take advantage of the economies of scale offered for high-volume transmission over digital, bulk-transmission links. This situation will not change until a PL offering is developed that can serve as a common gate for all of these transmission forms, enabling the mingled, digitized messages to be sent over one common link.

The cross-over from piecemeal connection to an integrated network should occur when the mechanism for integration becomes cost-effective. The complexity that can be eliminated through integration and the increased services that integration can make available should be considered when determining cost-effectiveness.

The special transmission requirements of data (higher speeds, improved reliability, greater capacity) have already revolutionized the carrier industry

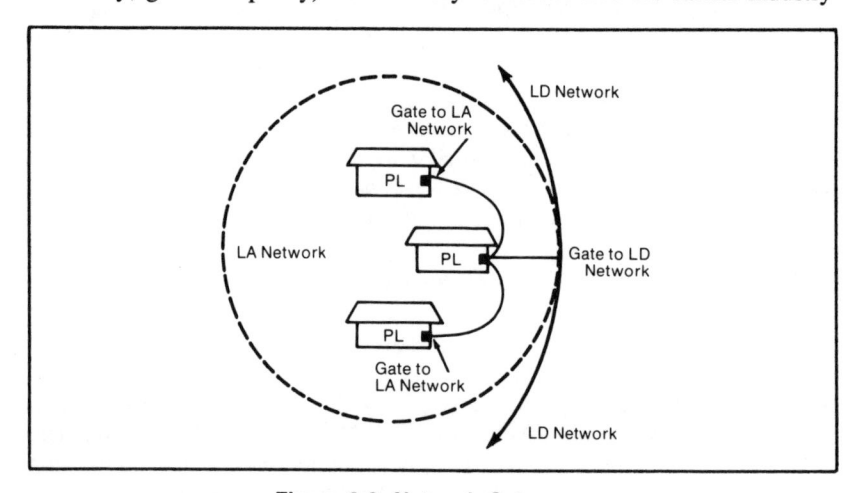

Figure 8-2. Network Gates

DESIGNING AN INTEGRATED NETWORK

and have effectively separated the transmission forms into two groups: one including voice, fax, Telex, and other high-tolerance, slow transmissions; the other including only data. Video transmissions, ranging from still-images to full-motion teleconferencing, have some characteristics of both types of transmission. Video's high tolerances make it suitable for transmission over voice links, but its requirements for high speeds and high capacity make it too expensive for voice lines. Broadband transmission links (e.g., satellite and microwave links) appear to be the most likely medium for teleconferencing, since these links satisfy the cost and capacity requirements for video.

Communications technologies have achieved successful integration at the higher (LD) level. Carriers used LD links to carry digitized voice, data, and some video transmissions during the 1970s. The integration technologies are proceeding from LD to LA to PL, solving the macro problems first at the carrier level. At the lower levels, the problem becomes more complex because the distribution of the digitized messages becomes more refined. The problem is most difficult at the PL level, where the transmission flow must be broken down to each specific device (e.g., CRT, telephone, fax copier, word processor).

As the preceding paragraphs indicate, today's network design process is taking place in a period of transition. The designer's motto should be "prepared and waiting"; the organization must be ready to recognize and take advantage of the future offerings that will lead to simplification, greater manageability, and efficient use of bulk transmission links. Today, the designer must contend with a PL design similar to that in Figure 8-3 but must prepare for one such as that represented in Figure 8-4.

LA Networks

The future may bring direct premise-to-premise communications by satellite, eliminating the need for local area design; however, as long as the cost of premise satellite controllers is higher than that of terrestrial links, there will be a need for LA design.

Because of the state of the art in current systems, local-area network design is not a straightforward process. There are many options for LA networks, and there is always more than one way to accomplish a connection. There are also situations where a particular link (e.g., microwave) can be used in one location but not in others because of interference from buildings and clogging of bandwidths in metropolitan areas. The principle of seeking the advantages of bulk transmission is still a guideline for design; however, implementing this principle is difficult because of the alternatives available and the varying requirements of the particular organization. The underlying design strategy for LA networks is a repeated break-even analysis comparing bulk transmission facilities and shared carrier facilities.

The basic problems in LA network design are illustrated in Figure 8-5. The LA design process includes three phases. First, the limits of the local area must be defined. These limits are determined through a cost comparison of the

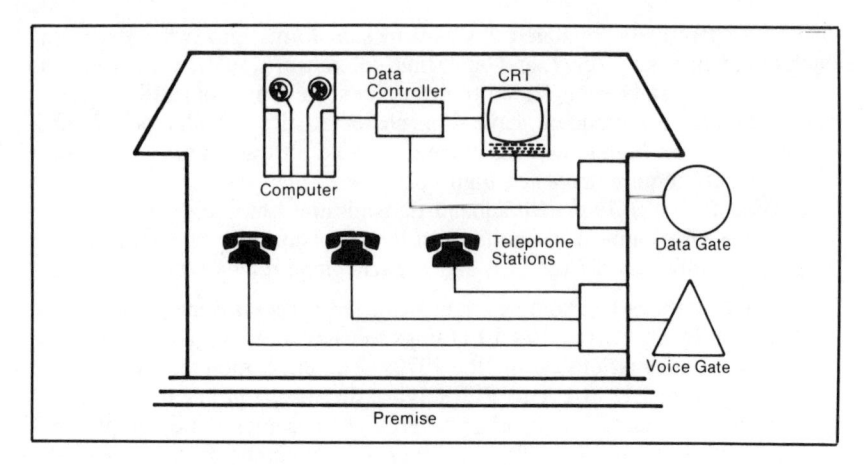

Figure 8-3. Separate Voice and Data Gates

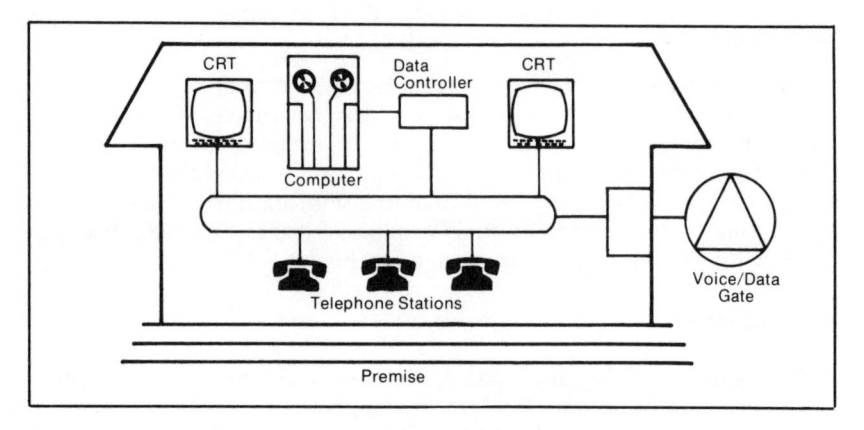

Figure 8-4. Integrated Voice/Data Gate

use of local-area communications and LD links for a certain location. A local area usually consists of an area with a radius of 25 miles, centered around a metropolitan area. A local area containing three premise locations is shown in Figure 8-6. Two premises have separate voice and data gates, and one has an integrated voice and data gate.

Each premise area sends and receives local and long-distance transmissions in both the voice and data ranges. Private links or shared carrier links can be used for premise-to-premise transmissions. The choice of link should be based on cost and on the services desired. The graph in Figure 8-6 shows the basic break-even analysis that should be performed for each connection. When the volume of transmission between two premises is so large that the price per unit of the private link is as low as that of the shared carrier link, the use of private links should be considered. Constantly climbing LA rates make this analysis even more critical.

DESIGNING AN INTEGRATED NETWORK 107

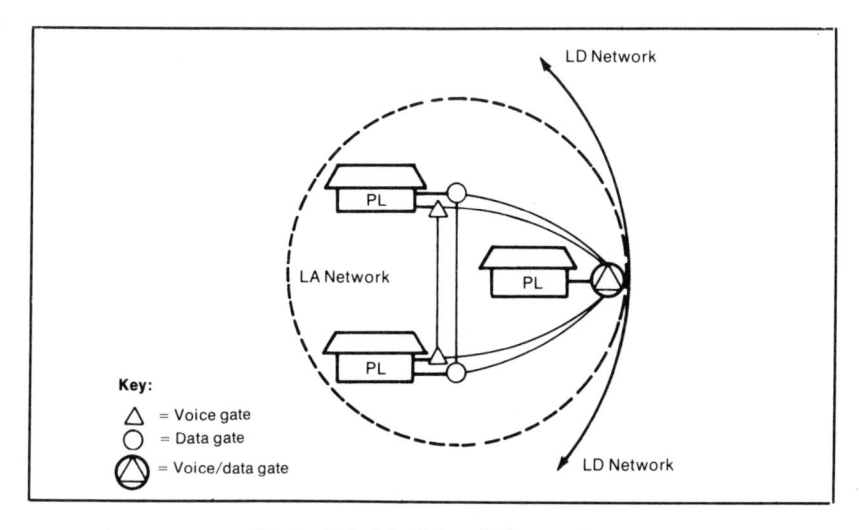

Figure 8-5. LA Network Connections

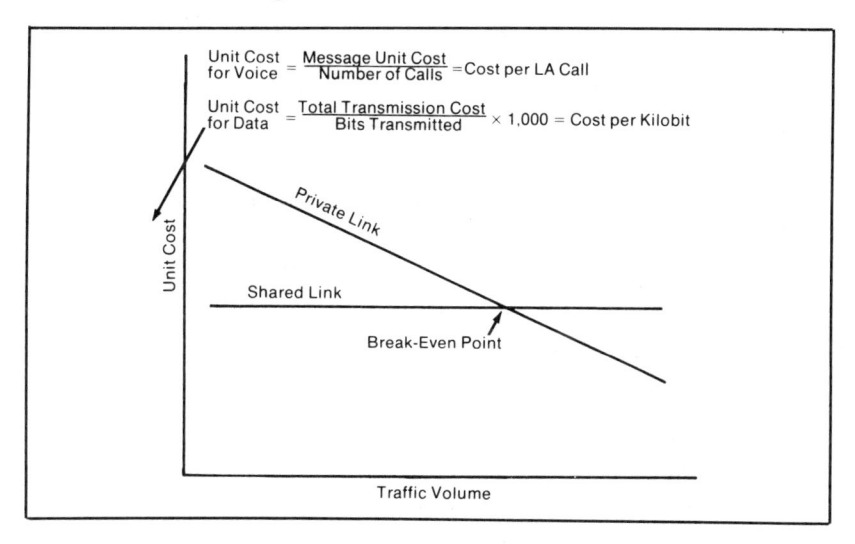

Figure 8-6. Break-Even Analysis for LA Networks

In the second phase of the LA analysis, the LA network should be analyzed in connection with the LD network. A private link between two premises in a local area may not be justified by local traffic between the two nodes; however, if substantial LD traffic from one node can be routed through the other node, a private link may be cost-effective. This is especially true if the local area is selected as a network node (i.e., a major network switching center) in the LD network.

The third phase of LA design applies only to premises that are close together. In general, it is easier and less expensive to use private links when premises are in close proximity. Buildings in a complex are easily connected through terrestrial links, microwave, or even light beams. Proximity also enables the use of telephone company voice offerings that make feasible the consolidation of several premises into one facility.

This 3-step LA analysis is applicable to voice and data transmission, whether separately or jointly. The development of effective, integrated voice and data transmission in LA networks hinges on vendor development of integrated PL systems. Once such systems are standardized, one premise will be able to communicate with another through a single voice/data gate. Until an integrated system is developed, the LA network area may consist of separate transmission links for each transmission form.

LD Networks

The word "telecommunications" usually evokes thoughts of long-distance networks. As the previous discussion shows, this should not be the case. In the past, however, LD networking has received more attention than the other two areas because of the growing need for data transmission and the high cost associated with LD. The situation has changed considerably; competition in the LD market and the greater capacities of LD transmission links (T-carriers, satellites, waveguides, microwave) have caused LD rates to drop significantly. As a result, LD is several steps ahead of LA and PL in networking state of the art.

The basic LD design methodology follows these steps:
- Identify traffic patterns between local areas.
- Identify projected traffic growth, and superimpose those projections on current traffic patterns.
- Identify corporate location preferences.
- Establish network nodes.

As mentioned previously, the network nodes are major switching points. The voice and data networks will not necessarily be aligned in one design; however, the nodes for each network can be selected to facilitate later integration. The technology that will make integration feasible is developing from the LD area downward; this makes LD a prime choice for pilot programs on voice/data integration.

CONCLUSION

Two basic recommendations follow from the previous discussion. First, the network design process must be separated from the concerns of each transmission form. Network design must satisfy the requirements of all transmission forms needed by the business. Second, the design should facilitate the use of bulk transmission links where possible. This strategy will help bring about the integration of voice and data while optimizing the cost-effectiveness of the facilities.

Telecommunications technologies are still in the early stages of development and lack maturity. The 1980s will see the development of integrated networks combining all transmission forms, and designing a network with these strategies in mind can help an organization prepare for integrated transmission.

9 Protocols and Compatibility for Distributed Processing

by James W. Conard

INTRODUCTION

Whether installing a new network or expanding an existing one, the DDP manager may need to integrate a variety of heterogeneous equipment, systems, and facilities into a smoothly functioning, cohesive network that will satisfy user requirements. Network components are often provided by different hardware and software vendors; even facilities may be provided by different communications common carriers. These suppliers are likely to have their own architectures, interface requirements, and unique characteristics. The manager is faced with various potential compatibility issues.

Identifying these issues, planning to minimize their impact, and the efforts of the standards community to resolve them are the focus of this chapter. The two fundamental categories of compatibility, communications control and message control, are discussed in relationship to the DDP environment. The Reference Model for Open Systems Interconnection (OSI), recently published by the International Standards Organization (ISO), is described and used to put compatibility issues into perspective. The use of standardization as a tool that can, within limits, alleviate compatibility problems is also discussed.

The DDP Communications Environment

Communications is vital to the success of any distributed application, accounting for a significant part of the costs and the system resources. By definition, distributed applications must move information among an assortment of geographically dispersed processes resident in systems that range from simple asynchronous terminals to large computers. This information must be moved over communications media and facilities that may include anything from twisted-pair cable to satellite links and from local area networks to public data networks.

If this movement of information is to be successful, it is essential that the connected processes be compatible in two broad categories of communications-related functions: those involving the transport of data and those involving the content. These categories are shown in Figure 9-1. (Ap-

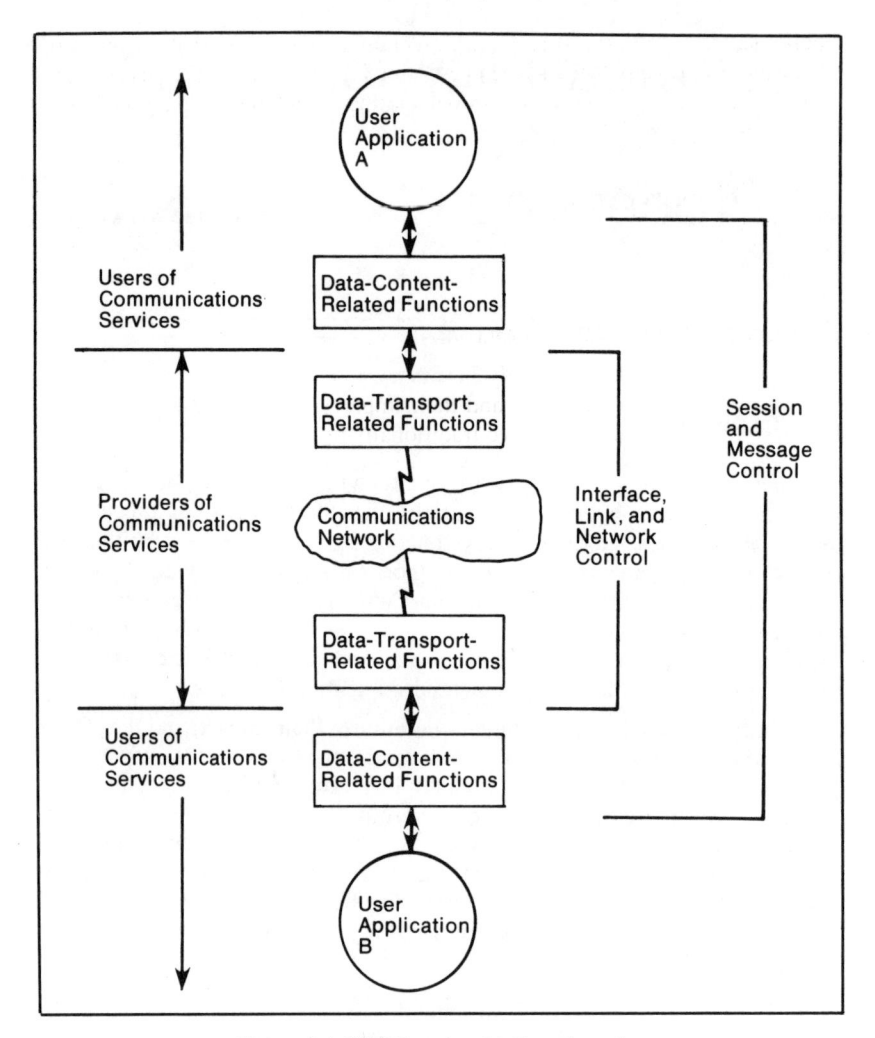

Figure 9-1. DDP Communications Levels

plication compatibility must also exist, but application-to-application issues are beyond the scope of this chapter.)

Data Transport. The functions related to the transport of data are concerned solely with the movement of a unit of data from point A to point B through two or more network nodes. Transport functions are no more concerned with the content or structure of the data than the postal service is with the contents of an envelope. Communications protocols at this level are, in fact, specifically designed to be totally transparent. High-level data link control (HDLC), advanced data communications control protocol (ADCCP), and synchronous data link control (SDLC) are typical protocols. Data transport functions include control of the communications facility interface; control of one or more intervening links to ensure reliable, error-free data delivery; and control of the network to provide proper routing, flow control, data blocking, and so on.

Data Content. The functions related to the content of data are directly concerned with its format and structure as well as with administration and control of the connection or session (whether permanent or temporary) between two application processes. These higher-level functions are also directly involved with presentation format (screen display and printer output requirements) as well as with data interpretation and code transformation.

Information can flow smoothly between end-user applications only when these categories are compatible, and their important differences must be recognized. Transport functions have traditionally been the domain of the communicators, the providers of communications services, while the (architecturally) higher functions related to the data content are of more direct concern to the users of these services. (The definition of these functions and their segmentation into manageable layers was an impetus to the development of network architectures.)

NETWORK ARCHITECTURE

A distributed network is essentially a collection of processing systems interconnected by communications facilities. Portions of the application task are distributed among the cooperating systems; the necessary interchange of information is provided by the communications services. The network architecture is the formalized logical structure of the interactions and functions required to provide these services.

The explosive growth of communications networks, primarily in response to the demands of distributed processing, threatened to parallel the early chaotic development of link control protocols. Each manufacturer was developing a unique method of interconnecting its products that was, in general, incompatible with others. Each was called a network architecture; examples include Burroughs' Network Architecture (BNA), Digital Equipment's Digital Network Architecture (DNA), IBM's System Network Architecture (SNA), and NCR's Distributed Network Architecture (DNA).

Each of these architectures consists of a series of hierarchical layers that provide defined functions related to communications services. This is a common structure because it enables the functions and services of one layer to be isolated from those of another. The task of describing, designing, and implementing these functions is thus simplified.

ISO Reference Model

The proliferation of architectures suited to a specific manufacturer's view of the networking problem demonstrated a need for a unified approach to permit interconnection of heterogeneous systems. Such an architecture would permit a system to be open to all other systems complying with the rules of the architecture. The efforts of many people in the industry, working through the standards organizations, resulted in the development of the hierarchical structure known as ISO DP7498 Reference Model for Open Systems Interconnection. This is currently in the approval process as an international standard.

Conceptually, the model envisions the communications network as a number of entities connected by some physical medium. Each entity is composed of a logical series of successive layers (see Figure 9-2). Each layer interfaces with the layers above and below it and performs the functions necessary to provide a defined set of services to the layer above; it also requests services from the layer below. Each layer effectively isolates the implementation details of those below from those above. This isolation permits the characteristics of a layer to change without affecting the rest of the model, provided the services offered and requested do not change. A character-oriented protocol, for example, could be replaced by a bit-oriented protocol.

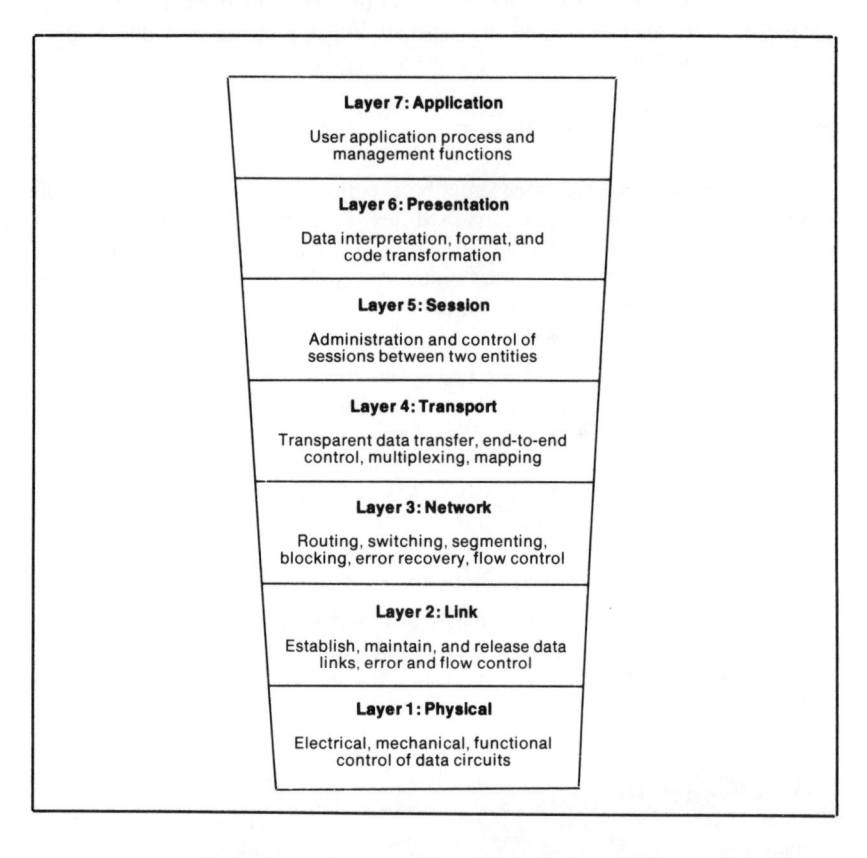

Layer 7: Application
User application process and management functions

Layer 6: Presentation
Data interpretation, format, and code transformation

Layer 5: Session
Administration and control of sessions between two entities

Layer 4: Transport
Transparent data transfer, end-to-end control, multiplexing, mapping

Layer 3: Network
Routing, switching, segmenting, blocking, error recovery, flow control

Layer 2: Link
Establish, maintain, and release data links, error and flow control

Layer 1: Physical
Electrical, mechanical, functional control of data circuits

Figure 9-2. Communications Control Hierarchy

PROTOCOLS AND COMPATIBILITY

Service requests, other parameters, control information, and data are transferred across the interfaces. A peer-to-peer protocol relationship also exists with the corresponding layer in a connected system or an intermediate network node (if required). These relationships are shown in Figure 9-3. The model illustrates the 2-level compatibility problem described earlier. The lower physical, link, network, and transport layers are a finer division of the data transport function shown in Figure 9-1. The higher session, presentation, and application layers are subdivisions of the data-content-related functions.

The reference model is not a specific recommendation for solving any particular networking problem. Rather, it is an organized means of segmenting and codifying communications functions in a universally applicable manner and has already found wide industry acceptance. Standards bodies throughout the world are currently generating standards for each of the levels. These activities are described in the following sections of this chapter.

DATA TRANSPORT COMPATIBILITY ISSUES

At the levels concerned with transport, the problem is the movement of data among geographically dispersed application processes. Communications networks evolved to solve the geographic problem. Different requirements, however, inevitably led to the development of different types of networks. The venerable public switched telephone network was used early for data communications; it has carried and will probably continue to carry significant volumes of data. Private data networks using dedicated common-carrier facilities provide the advantages of constant availability, better reliability, and higher throughput but do so at relatively high cost. Both circuit- and packet-switched public networks evolved, in many respects, in response to the demands of distributed processing requirements. Recently, local area networks have emerged to meet the need for high data capacity, multiple connections, and no centralized control in a closely knit local community.

Although communications networks solve the geographic problem by linking remote processing facilities, they do create additional compatibility problems. As shown in Figure 9-4, any constituent part of the distributed system may have to contend with the interface, protocols, and characteristics of several types of networks to accomplish its objectives.

The variety of available communications facilities represents only one-half of the potential compatibility problem. The DDP manager must also consider the characteristics of the hardware and software components that comprise the network's nodes and processing facilities. These also have interfunction interfaces, protocols, system parameters, and items subject to bilateral agreement that are likely to cause difficulty. This is especially true when more than one vendor is involved or when an existing network is being expanded by the addition of new equipment.

If potential compatibility problems can be identified, they can be overcome, or their impact can, at least, be minimized by planning and careful attention to detail. A major obstacle is the difficulty of recognizing the points

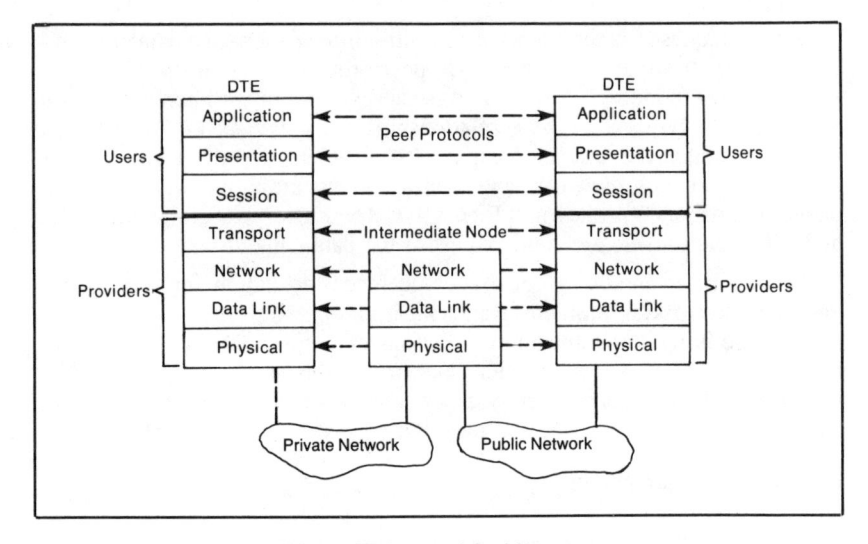

Figure 9-3. Layered Architecture

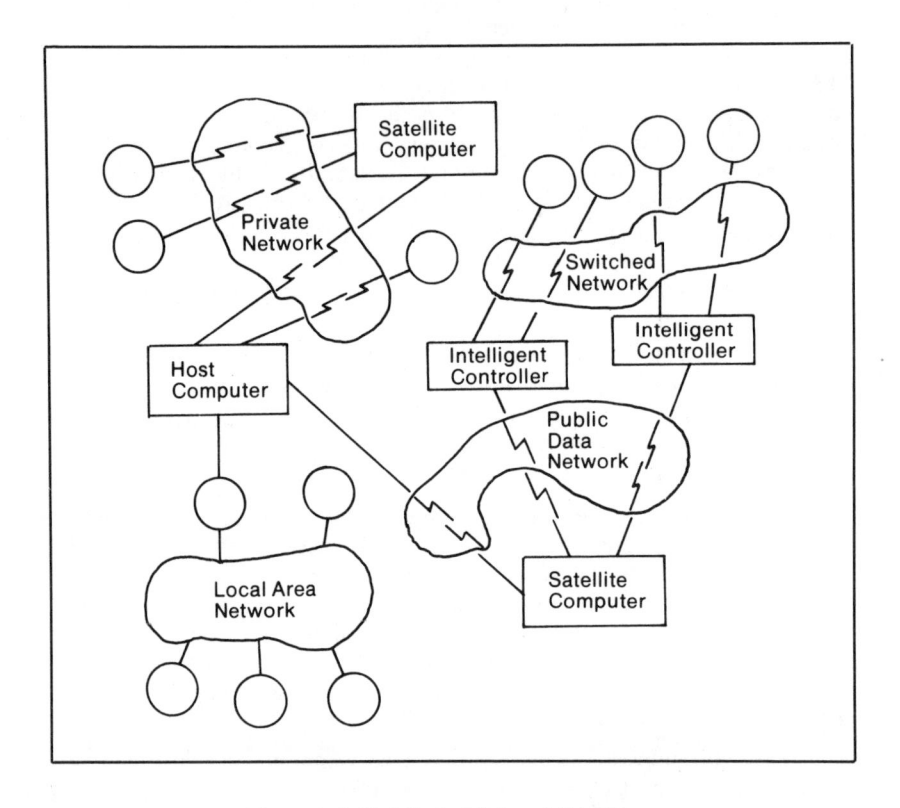

Figure 9-4. Distributed Network Facilities

PROTOCOLS AND COMPATIBILITY

at which compatibility problems may arise in a very complex flow of information. In such cases, the ISO reference model can be a valuable tool. Its segmented structure can be used to divide the problem into manageable parts, each of which can be examined for potential issues. The reference model has segmented the transport-related functions into four layers: physical, link, network, and transport (as shown in Figure 9-2). These layers allow identification of compatibility issues at each level.

Physical Layer

Compatibility issues at the physical layer are those most directly concerned with the interface characteristics of the communications medium or facility. This layer contains the protocols that govern the electrical, mechanical, functional, and procedural interchanges with the many different network types. Compatibility problems here are usually focused in a single tangible interface (e.g., a connector to a modem), making them the easiest to identify. In addition, this interface has probably received the most attention in terms of standardization. Nevertheless, the manager must be aware of the following potential problems:

- The choice of an interface standard from the many promulgated by CCITT and EIA or from such de facto standards as AT&T's.
- The exact definition of electrical characteristics, including wave shapes, voltage levels, balanced or unbalanced mode, and even signal and equipment grounding methods.
- The definition of subsets of available functions.
- Procedural compatibility in signal sense (e.g., true/false, on/off); these must not be taken for granted.
- Precise definition of time-outs. A lack of understanding or inadequate planning of time-out functions can cause great difficulty.
- Mechanical problems related to which side of the interface has the female connector and such seemingly mundane items as who provides the cable and in what length.
- Facility characteristics such as two- or four-wire, half- or full-duplex, and any required facility conditioning.

These items do not exhaust all possible compatibility problems; they do, however, indicate the potential for difficulty even at a level as seemingly well defined as the physical level.

Link Layer

The link layer protocol is a key element in the success of a distributed network. Choices here establish the rules and formats for the interchange of data throughout the network community. Link layer protocols govern the establishment of the link, control of information and supervisor transfers, termination of the exchange, and recovery from abnormal conditions.

Several similar (but not completely compatible) data link control protocols have evolved during the past several years. These bit-oriented protocols are

expected to gradually replace the older character-oriented protocols. Even though these protocols are well documented and well defined, the potential for compatibility problems is still present; including:
- The initial choice of a data link protocol—The choice is heavily influenced by the networking facilities in use (public or private data, dedicated or switched). The choice may be predetermined by the selection of terminal equipment, since most manufacturers choose and design into the equipment one of the commonly used protocols. The possible variations in implementation can be a major source of compatibility problems.
- The class of procedure to be used—HDLC (a bit-oriented protocol) offers a choice of three basic classes of link control.
- The options and functional subset choices—HDLC, as an example, offers 11 defined functional extensions from which to choose. Between the choice of class and the choice of options, this one protocol has 33 defined variables. The potential for compatibility problems is obvious.
- The initialization procedures—Potential issues here include the need for initialization on power-up or reinitialization after power failure as well as the requirement for downline load and accompanying procedure, format, and verification.
- The maximum length of blocks or frames of data—Incompatibilities often arise because stations send longer blocks of data than the buffers of the receiving station can handle.
- The addressing schemes—Station addresses may be hard-wired or programmable in various forms. They may be unique to a link, unique within a network, or universally unique. They may be fixed or variable in length or predefined by protocol, as in X.25.
- The byte (or character) alignment of data—Some protocols permit data to be any number of bits in any code. Others require that data be aligned on a byte, character, or octet boundary.
- The system parameter values—Every link protocol has many parameters with values subject to bilateral agreement. These range from timer values and the number of attempts at retransmission to actions for recovery from abnormal conditions.

Network Layer

The network layer contains the protocols that manage the routing and flow of data through the network, which may consist of tandem links. The network layer also manages the segmenting and blocking of data, sequencing, and network-level error detection and recovery. Because of the predominance of the X.25 protocol, this level is often referred to as the packet level. As with the lower link and physical layers, the network layer has many potential areas of compatibility difficulty. Among these are:
- Flow control mechanisms are often provided at the network layer that permit receiving nodes or terminals to regulate the flow of data when it threatens to exceed capacity. The need for flow control, its impact on

PROTOCOLS AND COMPATIBILITY

other nodes, and techniques for implementation are often an issue. If flow mechanisms are used, they must be well understood and compatible.
- Network connectors are used at this layer to transfer data. These connections or circuits can be dedicated point-to-point or multipoint, or they can use the general switched network. Each has its own requirements for setup, maintenance, and termination of the connection.
- In a packet network, choices and issues related to the use of virtual calls or permanent virtual circuits must be resolved. Although virtual calls exist only for their duration, they require overhead related to call setup and termination. Permanent virtual circuits behave much like dedicated circuits in a private network.
- Expediting data delivery is another network layer issue, which can mean a priority scheme for certain blocks. In a packet network, datagrams, fast select procedures, or both may have to be evaluated. These provide a means of rapid packet delivery at reduced overhead but with many restrictions on such issues as reliability of delivery.
- Multiplexing several network connections onto a single data link is possible in some implementations. The procedural implications, however, may affect compatibility.
- Internetwork protocols are an issue at the network layer. Unless the distributed network is composed entirely of dedicated facilities, it is likely that the data traffic may have to transmit over more than one network. This is virtually certain if international traffic is involved and raises a number of compatibility issues.

Transport Layer

The transport layer is the highest of the four levels directly concerned with transmitting data through the network. This layer is intended to provide services that bridge the gap between those provided by the network layer and those required by the session layer. This layer thus provides a full-duplex line for the exchange of data between processes in connected systems.

The issues related to this layer are more philosophical than practical. Such questions as the precise boundary between the session and transport layers and whether the transport layer is needed at all remain unsettled. There is some argument that transport layer functions can be performed at the network layer.

DATA CONTENT COMPATIBILITY ISSUES

The three upper layers of the hierarchical structure shown in Figure 9-2 are concerned with the content of data and the existence of logical connections between processes to transfer this data. They are rarely involved in the physical activity associated with moving the data because such activity is transparent to these levels. Many believe that the realm of DP, as contrasted with data communications, is entered at these levels.

Compatibility issues at the upper levels are far more nebulous and difficult to define. It is normal for protocols in this area to be entirely within the software structure and intimately related to the machine architecture. Thus, it is sometimes difficult for the distributed network manager to identify and quantify interfaces. Furthermore, little effort has been devoted to generating standards for these layers. Such efforts are now being initiated, however, and are discussed in the following sections.

Session Layer

A session is a cooperative relationship between two entities that facilitates the transfer of data between them. For example, the relationship that exists between a terminal operator and the remote data base being accessed is called a session. The session layer of the model exists to provide services related to the administration, establishment, maintenance, and termination of this dialogue. The issues most likely to cause compatibility problems in this layer are the procedural elements involved in setting up sessions (e.g., location of applications, resource allocation, authorization for access, and security checks).

Presentation Layer

The presentation layer interprets the meaning of data for the application layer. It is concerned with the formatting and transformations necessary to convert raw data into an image for a printer or display screen. This level is the focus of the myriad compatibility problems arising from communications between dissimilar devices. The application expects all differences among devices to be normalized, absorbed, eliminated, or translated. Such universal device transparency can be very complex, highly restrictive, or impossible. Compatibility issues at this level obviously require a great deal of attention.

Application Layer

The highest layer of the model is the application layer. The issues are those related to interfaces to user application processes and those dealing with overall management of communications services provided by the lower levels. It is important to note that the application layer does not represent the user's application. It is instead the user's means for accessing the communications services provided by the network.

Although this discussion has addressed compatibility issues in terms of layers, it should not be assumed that the layered structure is engraved on a stone tablet. It must be stressed that the most significant characteristic of an architecture is not its internal organization or the location of specific functions; it is its external behavior as perceived by an interconnected system. The potential compatibility issues discussed in this chapter, although not exhaustive, should alert the DDP manager to the kinds of problems that can arise and the kinds of information and resources needed to combat them. One of the primary tools is communications standards.

COMMUNICATIONS STANDARDS

Familiarity with communications standards and their application to the distributed processing environment can be a distinct asset to the DDP manager. By serving as a common reference point, standards can resolve facility and equipment interface problems and simplify the interconnection of heterogeneous systems.

The major communications standards and activities of interest to the DDP manager are discussed here as they relate to the architectural reference model. The primary standards-making bodies are the American National Standards Institute (ANSI), International Standards Organization (ISO), Electronic Industries Association (EIA), and the Consultative Committee on International Telegraph and Telephone (CCITT). The federal government, manufacturers, and professional groups (e.g., IEEE) are also deeply involved.

Physical Level. The physical level may be the key to successful implementation and operation of a distributed network, although the possibility for incompatibility is great. Fortunately, this level is also the best defined, with available and proven standards. Table 9-1 lists the most frequently used standards governing the interface between the terminal equipment and the facilities provided by the common carrier or network supplier. These standards define the electrical, mechanical, and functional characteristics of the interface. They provide the establishment and release of a connection and have fault-monitoring capability.

Table 9-1. Physical Layer Interface Standards

EIA	ANSI	CCITT	ISO	Federal Standard
RS-422		X.27, V.11		1020A
RS-423		X.26, V.10		1030A
RS-449		V.24, V.10	DP4902	1031
	Proposed ANSI X.21	X.21, X.24	DP4903	1040
RS-232C		V.24, V.28	DP2110	

Link Level. At the link level, IBM's Binary Synchronous Communications (BSC), in all its variations, is the best-known character-oriented standard. The major bit-oriented link control standards that are now coming into widespread use are ANSI's advanced data communications control procedures (ADCCP), ISO's high-level data link control (HDLC), and CCITT's X.25 line access procedure (LAPB).

Application of these protocols will greatly ease compatibility problems in controlling the transfer of data through the network. The manager must remain concerned, however, with proper selection of options and system parameters.

Network Level. The best-known network layer standard is CCITT's X.25. This is generated as a standard for interfacing public data networks but is often used for point-to-point dedicated links. X.25 spans the three lower layers of the reference model. At level 1 it specifies X.21 or X.21 *bis* (equivalent to RS-232C); at level 2 it uses a link access procedure compatible with the HDLC subset. Level 3 is the packet-level protocol.

Although formal published standards for the higher layers of the model are scarce, this situation will change rapidly. Intensive work by ISO, CCITT, and ANSI will result in transport, session, and presentation layer standards. AT&T has recently published a version of a network communications protocol called BX.25. This contains an excellent description of a session layer protocol that encompasses levels 4, 5, and 6 of the reference model.

Other Standards

The National Bureau of Standards has launched a major program to develop high-level standards. The objective is to define transport, session, presentation, and application layer protocols as well as internetwork protocols during the next several years.

Many ancillary standards are also of interest to distributed application network managers. ANSI, EIA, and the federal government have issued standards dealing with code sets, signaling rates, encryption, performance, and performance measurement. Communications standards will not resolve every compatibility issue, but their judicious application can help to reduce the number and severity of such issues. In addition, their widespread availability can ease product procurement, and their high level of compatibility can reduce development time. Standards are a most useful tool in cost-effective network implementation and management.

10 Information Confidentiality in Distributed Systems

by John R. Kessler

INTRODUCTION

Distributed processing is now past the theoretical stage; many operating distributed systems now exist, and industry journals and seminars are full of case studies that scrutinize and evaluate these systems. As with all new technologies, successes and failures occur in DDP. Actual implementations are uncovering significant issues that were either glossed over or ignored during the theoretical stage. DDP raises a variety of challenging issues—technical, economical, political, functional, and even social.

One such issue is information confidentiality, which includes the subjects of privacy and security. The distinctions and relationships among these three areas must be understood:
- Information is *private* when it is known only by one individual.
- When private information is shared with another, *confidentiality* is required.
- To ensure confidentiality, *security* measures must be implemented.

Information confidentiality, therefore, is a need that is met operationally through security. This chapter will examine various techniques for providing information confidentiality in DDP systems.

The Need for Confidentiality

Since the concept of data as a corporate resource emerged during the 1970s, efficient management of this resource has been emphasized. DDP can increase efficiency in managing the data resource by providing the following:
- Improved reliability
- Improved availability
- Improved response times
- Control of data at operating points

When these objectives are realized, the data resource contributes more to the organization.

DDP involves decentralization of processing, which, in turn, requires a decentralization of the data resource. The requirements for protecting the confidentiality of data in a distributed environment are thus more complex.

When the processing, transmission, and storage of data are automated, three factors are introduced that must be considered in order to ensure information confidentiality. First, the data is stored in some form of data file. This can range from punched cards and magnetic strips to such complex forms of data organization as data bases. Whatever the storage method, if the data being stored is confidential, data file protection is necessary.

Second, once data is stored in a data file, it requires manipulation by computer programs. In some cases these programs contain processing logic formulas that are confidential. In such instances the programs themselves may require controls in order to ensure protection.

Third, data is transported in various modes, from shipment of magnetic tapes to complex telecommunications networks. Confidentiality must be ensured in transport as well as in storage and operation.

What must be protected is summarized in the following list:
- Data
- Data transmission
- Data maintenance
- Data access
- Computer data files
- Computer programs

An analysis of confidentiality requirements should follow the sequence of this list. For example, if the data involved is not sensitive in itself, it is unlikely that the data transmission will require controls. Guidelines should be provided to ensure that an overkill of confidentiality controls does not lessen the cost-effectiveness of a DDP application.

The analysis of actual DDP implementations provides insight into their successes or failures. Frequently, the major cause of failure is lack of control. Control is a value-laden term—to many it means project development delay, user inconvenience, and additional processing or staffing costs. Control also has the unpleasant connotations of restriction and enforcement. Such attitudes are self-defeating, however; when viewed positively, control can contribute to success. In any case, control is necessary in order to ensure information confidentiality in the distributed environment.

Data can be compromised because of mistakes, natural disaster, sabotage, or criminal activity. The following are a few representative examples of classes of business data that must be protected from compromise:
- Employee information
- Customer information
- Financial information
- Supplier ratings
- Future product design
- Market strategy
- Research techniques

When information is compromised, it is often difficult to quantify the adverse effects. Compromise may result in poor employee morale, loss of

INFORMATION CONFIDENTIALITY

competitive edge in product announcement or market penetration, customer dissatisfaction, lawsuits, and so on. Breaches in confidentiality caused by lack of proper controls can have serious effects on the DP department as well: DDP is still a new technology, and such adverse effects can undermine the organization's confidence in the concept.

To ensure that the cost advantages of DDP are fully realized, controls must be used prudently. The security measures discussed in this chapter should not be applied to all DDP applications. A thorough analysis of business requirements and a careful consideration of all available approaches are necessary in order to develop practical and effective confidentiality controls.

ORGANIZATION AND CONTROLS

As a DDP application emerges, confidentiality requirements must be analyzed. Planners should decide what information should be protected. Only after this question is thoroughly explored should developers consider how the information should be protected. In many DDP applications, there will be no confidentiality requirements; in such cases, the overhead of unnecessary protection should be avoided.

What to Protect

When determining what information should be protected, the first analysis should focus on application data. There are various levels of confidentiality; different types of data may require different controls (e.g., payroll data may be handled differently from affirmative action data). Collection of data on hours worked by employees for payroll purposes is a typical use of DDP that may require little or no confidentiality control.

In the manufacturing industry, new-product design is a candidate for confidentiality protection. Graphic design data is rapidly becoming a major resource in large organizations. This technology allows the engineering designer to utilize the advantages of DDP for daily tasks. When new design data must be transmitted by way of telecommunication links for use by other engineers in the corporation, confidentiality becomes a problem. Years of research on a new product design must not be jeopardized during transmission.

A corporation's financial data, especially inventory data, may be maintained by a DDP application at an operating unit and periodically transmitted for summarization and preparation for financial analysis at the central DP facility. While in many cases the final analysis becomes public record in stockholder and government reports, the timing of the release of such information may be critical to financing negotiations, stock-market offerings, and so on. In such cases summarized data may require protection.

Electronic mail and office automation are included in the realm of DDP in some organizations. Here, also, the sensitivity of the data being transmitted and/or stored must be analyzed in order to determine confidentiality requirements.

The maintenance and inquiry functions should also be considered when determining the confidentiality controls needed for a DDP application. The type of control required is often determined by the distinction between these two functions. Maintenance is often performed by fewer users than is inquiry and, therefore, may be easier to control. Wide data access through inquiry can have many advantages; however, if not adequately controlled, the inquiry function can be a cause of poor business decisions. For example, product failure data is sometimes collected for reliability analysis in order to aid in making subsequent engineering improvements. Such analysis is often done statistically, using market or geographic locations and a limited product population. Product and reliability engineers are familiar with the data being analyzed and the equations used in preparing reports and graphs. Marketing personnel, however, are not as well trained at interpreting this data. Premature access to the data by marketing personnel can lead to misinterpretations, which, in turn, can result in inaccurate market forecasts and invalid manufacturing capacity planning.

Organizational Changes

To create a DDP environment with a good reputation for confidentiality, a company must first make organizational changes that define security responsibilities and establish controls that are understood, accepted, and realistic. It is essential that these controls are accepted; if functional management, DDP developers, and end users do not cooperate in maintaining confidentiality, there will be many needless delays in DDP development, and the quality of the delivered product will probably reflect the lack of cooperation.

The Security Office. The first organizational step is the establishment of a DDP security office, which should provide administrative policies, standards, guidelines, and procedures for the necessary controls. The office should also provide security services during the implementation of controls. The service aspect of the office is important; as stated previously, security is the operational side of confidentiality. Few organizations have formally recognized security services. A purely administrative DDP security office would probably lead to confusion and confrontations and thus prove ineffective.

Personnel for the DDP security office should be selected carefully. They must have the respect and confidence of the organization they are charged with protecting. At the same time, they must know enough about DDP to avoid being overwhelmed by technical restrictions that may only be excuses. Unfortunately, few individuals meet these requirements.

The individual(s) selected for the security office must also know when to be firm and when to compromise. An overzealous confidentiality officer will stunt DDP growth, while a weak individual can defeat the entire purpose of the office. In any case, the position is advisory and will be unpopular at times, especially if the office is not supported by senior management and is not well understood by operating management.

Depending on the size and complexity of the organization, the security office staff can range from one individual, who may also have other responsibilities, to a central corporate staff and distributed site officers. The primary role of this staff is to act as a liaison between user management and DDP developers. The security office staff must be capable of appraising business needs and relating them to DDP technical considerations. Specific duties of the DDP security officer(s) will be outlined in the section entitled Control Alternatives.

The following list provides some guidelines about the required qualifications for a DDP security officer:
- Minimum qualifications:
  —From one to two years of technical design in system areas (e.g., systems software, telecommunications, or data base architecture)
  —From two to three years of application analysis, preferably in functional areas of the organization where DDP is anticipated
  —From one to two years of consulting with DDP vendors and with other companies employing DDP, as well as attendance at seminars on DDP issues
  —Supervisory or management responsibilities and demonstrated ability to motivate employees, to listen, and to recognize when to consider alternatives and compromises
- Further qualifications (if possible):
  —Actual experience in the functional areas to be served
  —Time spent on both operating and corporate staffs
  —An awareness of or actual experience in the total systems planning function

The reporting position of the security officer(s) depends on the organization. The position is staff and administrative and will also provide services. In any case, the function should be independent of the managers in charge of DDP development.

An additional challenge for security officers and others responsible for confidentiality controls is staying current with the ever-changing DDP technology. Time and funds must be allotted to allow these individuals to attend trade seminars and visit other companies. Access to trade journals and training programs for new personnel are also necessary.

EDP Auditing. A second organizational consideration is the EDP auditing function. Most organizations currently have some form of EDP auditing. Auditing was not applied to DP until relatively late in the history of the computing industry, and the auditing function has been playing catch-up ever since. Rapid technological growth has made the auditor's job difficult. DDP developers can learn from this fact and consider the auditing issue from the start.

The auditing department must work closely with the security office. When confidentiality controls are developed and implemented, follow-through for verification by the auditing staff is essential. They must ensure that requirements recognized during development are met after implementation. To support the efforts of the security office and keep the auditing staff informed, the DDP developers must include personnel from these staffs in the system development effort.

Developing Controls

The crucial development phase for information confidentiality is the definition phase. During this phase, user requirements are developed, vendor selection considered, and return on investment (ROI) calculated. Both vendor selection and ROI will be affected by information confidentiality requirements. If DDP hardware and software are selected before confidentiality is discussed, the equipment may not meet confidentiality requirements.

Implementing confidentiality controls may increase operational costs and thus affect ROI. A careful analysis of business requirements should be carried out in order to determine the confidentiality requirements. The details of the analysis should be presented with the ROI statement as supportive information, stating both the tangible and intangible benefits of the controls.

During this analysis, the security officer should work with user management in order to determine what information must be protected. Once the confidentiality requirements are specified, the DDP developers are responsible for implementing any necessary controls.

Project Review Meeting. The DDP developers should consider the control alternatives, prepare a preliminary system design, and prepare development and operational cost estimates for the ROI analysis. To ensure that the definition phase is complete, a project review meeting should be held before proceeding with the design phase of the project. Such a review should encompass development strategy, timetables, and estimated costs. Management must approve the plans before the project can continue.

This review is most successful if administered in a parliamentarian manner by a neutral party. The following personnel should participate in the review:
- Functional user
- DDP project leader
- Security officer (if confidentiality needs have been identified)

The following personnel should be invited to observe the review:
- Computer auditors
- Operations representative
- Software representative
- DDP project analyst/programmers
- Security officer (if there are no confidentiality needs)

The primary objective of this review is communication among numerous affected parties concerning an upcoming DDP implementation. The functional user and DDP project leader share the responsibility of presenting the scope and direction of the project. Discussion by invitees should be encouraged. Formal minutes should be published. If significant issues are raised during the review, they should be documented and assigned a date for resolution. Appropriate follow-up should be ensured.

Final sign-off on the proposed implementation should be required from both functional management and the security office. A formal document should be used for this sign-off, and a copy should be forwarded to the auditing staff in order to alert them to future auditing requirements.

CONTROL ALTERNATIVES

The type of control chosen depends on user requirements. The following controls are available to facilitate confidentiality:
- Physical controls
- User IDs, passwords, and security profiles
- Data partitioning
- Encryption

Physical Controls

Physical controls are measures that control physical access to DDP hardware. At the simplest level this may involve a surveillance camera that scans the DDP terminal room. The film would be monitored at specified intervals.

A terminal room can also be physically secured by security guards. If further sophistication is justified, automated recognition systems (e.g., badge readers, fingerprint readers, voice recognition systems) can be used.

The feasibility of physical controls depends on the structure of the DDP system. If the hardware for a given application is physically dispersed, physical controls are more costly and difficult to implement.

The cost of the various alternatives must also be considered. A security guard or even a door buzzer that must be rung in order to gain entry to the computer facility may be adequate. If the nature of the business requires numerous control centers, then an automated recognition system may be economically feasible. Such systems can support various DDP and MIS applications. If the automated recognition system will be used for a number of applications, it may become a separate project requiring involvement and direction from the security office. The project may actually become a security staff request, in which case the burden of cost justification is not carried by just one functional DDP project.

User IDs, Passwords, and Security Profiles

These three controls should be integrated into a triangular structure. Management empowers specific individuals to perform specific tasks and, acting through a staff control group, informs the computer system of these tasks. The user interacts with the computer to perform these tasks, and the computer employs the controls fed it by management to grant—or limit—access. The computer then returns reports that enable management to determine whether the controls are effective.

If management, users, and the computer are viewed as the intersecting lines of a triangle (see Figure 10-1), the user authorization system can be viewed as the lines that pass among them. The implementation or integration of user control requires three elements. Foremost is user identification. A user ID is unique to each individual within the restricted population of system "insiders." Second is the password, which differs from an ID—it is attached to a resource. User IDs authorize users because of *who they are*, a password because of *what they know*.

The third element required to tie together the user ID and password is the security profile, which is either resource or user oriented and correlates users and resources. An ID is meaningless unless it is empowered to do something; a resource secured by a password is useless unless someone knows the password. If a user authorization scheme begins with the profile, however, the computer system has a definition that incorporates identification and access. The ID and password combine to form a security code, enabling one character string to serve both purposes.

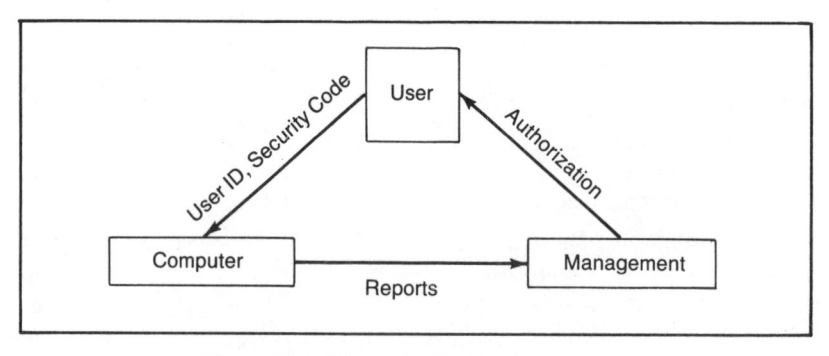

Figure 10-1. Triangular Control Structure

Establishing the Profile. When building these integrating elements, some practical matters must be considered. While constructing a resource profile is easier than is constructing a user profile, the latter is easier to maintain. For instance, to create a resource profile when a new DDP system is installed, the system managers need only define the resources involved and then correlate each with a list of authorized users. These users may be established categorically: all department members, all unit leaders, all senior officers, and so forth. These categories, however, do not hold firm. People leave, transfer, and are promoted. The maintenance task in such cases necessitates identifying all resources to which the individual had access. Certain employees have various levels of access to many systems, thus hindering thorough maintenance. For this reason, the additional effort involved in defining user profiles at time of system installation pays off handsomely in easier maintenance during the life of the system.

Assigning the User ID. After the profile is established, assigning the user ID follows. What is the ideal content and form of a user ID or password?

First, it must be unique; second, it must be sufficiently random that casual experimentation with spurious passwords will be unlikely to break system security. A good rule of thumb is that anything that occurs more often than one in two hundred cannot be dismissed as circumstantial. Thus, a 4-digit numeric identifier, with 10,000 possible variations, should not be used in a system having significantly more than 50 users. If, however, four alphanumeric characters are used for an identifier, there are 1,679,616 possible variations (36^4 [10 digits, 26 letters]). Studies show that users tend to confuse the letters "I" and "O" with the numbers one and zero; thus, it is advised that these letters not be used. This proscription leaves 1,336,336 combinations of 34 alphanumeric characters. Using the 200:1 rule, about 6,600 users could be accommodated.

Another important characteristic of the ideal password is memorability. Clearly, the shorter a password, the easier it is to remember. A shorter password, however, somewhat loses in randomness. If a password or user ID is too long for easy memorization, users almost invariably write it down and post it where it can be easily reached (e.g., on top of the terminal).

How long, then, is a character string that minimizes the trade-offs between randomness and memorability? In a recent study, nearly all participants could remember an alphanumeric character string of three, four, or five characters. With six or seven characters, only three out of four had accurate recall. At eight characters, only 17 percent could remember the string. Another portion of the test revealed that twice as many people exhibited long-term retention of a 5-character string as opposed to a 6-character string.

It is therefore recommended that no password exceed five randomly chosen alphanumeric characters. If randomness is maintained within the 200:1 range, five positions will permit 227,000 users. Thus, a 5-character alphanumeric password is ideal.

Stratification and Compartmentalization. Passwords and profiles are the skeleton of a user authorization system; they provide the means but not the substance to support a useful system. The substance of user authorization revolves around two managerial decisions: the degree of security that is to be associated with a given resource and the users who should be granted access to those resources. Together, both decisions determine any user authorization system.

Understanding the operating concepts involved in an online network is essential in making these decisions. All systems have a data base, even those lacking a formal package that performs data management functions. In this sense, a data base management system can be viewed in two parts: the data base is all information, in whatever form, necessary or available for operating the system; the management system is the sum of all functions of data capture, transmission, and use within the system. With these distinctions in mind, one can begin to construct a user authorization mechanism.

Stratification is one method of assigning security to system resources. The operative element is the transaction, or what the user may do. Activities are assigned a security level, or stratum. The extremes of stratification are that the individual may do nothing or may do everything. Compartmentalization, on the other hand, treats the data types as the operative elements. Thus, the definition must involve the types of security associated with particular access categories, or compartments, of the data base. The extremes in this scheme are access to nothing and access to everything.

Personnel Authorization. Having made the levels versus categories decision, management must then assign personnel to use the applications, preferably on a need-to-know basis. Each person should be given access to all information needed to perform the assigned job—neither more nor less.

Additional Controls. To further enhance control, user passwords or employee numbers entered into a DDP network from an authorized source can be subjected to a verification process. DDP terminals and/or control units can be restricted to particular departments. Periodic random prompting of users for identification can be implemented. When there is adequate knowledge of the job function being performed, session time can be restricted. Tight controls can be designed, but they usually become more costly as the required amount of control increases.

Auditing Procedures

To help the auditing staff with their tasks, audit trails are often required. Audit trails will increase development and operating costs and should therefore be justified by an analysis of business requirements. Performing periodic consistency audits for critical data is a more economical approach to confidentiality that will meet the needs of many applications. This audit function can be executed at random and thus has some advantages over in-process audit trails. This type of protection, however, is often remedial—a problem is identified and then corrected. Consistency audits should be used as the sole protection only in systems in which some confidentiality penetration can be tolerated.

Data Partitioning

Data partitioning is a design strategy that can be used in conjunction with other control alternatives. By creating subsets of data, access can be limited and confidentiality breaches minimized. Partitioning does not provide optimal protection, but it does reduce the cost of control. Partitioning also offers other benefits: in some DDP architectures, partitioned data can improve performance, simplify recovery, facilitate backup, and provide flexibility for future distribution of data.

Data Encryption

The confidentiality controls discussed thus far provide little protection against an intelligent penetration effort. Audit procedures may locate inten-

INFORMATION CONFIDENTIALITY

tional fraud but only after the fact, when some damage has probably already occurred. In addition, individuals who criminally penetrate a system are probably aware of the audit processes and will often take measures to circumvent discovery.

Most researchers in confidentiality agree that encryption is the most effective method for preventing the unauthorized disclosure of data. Even at this point, however, it must be understood that cryptography is not a complete solution and that there is still controversy over its use.

In general, encryption is the conversion of a message (plaintext) into seemingly meaningless form (ciphertext) through an algorithm. The encryption and decryption processes are controlled by a key. To date, cost justification of data encryption has been difficult. The rapidly declining costs of hardware are favorably changing this picture; however, encryption-key management often requires establishing or adding to a security staff, thus offsetting the cost reductions in hardware. If business conditions necessitate the use of an encryption system, careful study and planning should be conducted before implementing such a system. The encryption alternative selected may affect the hardware and system architecture chosen for the DDP network.

COMMON CONFIDENTIALITY OVERSIGHTS

As previously stated, confidentiality controls should be developed as part of the application development methodology. Even when this course is followed, however, common oversights may occur during development and after implementation.

Development Oversights

One of the most frequent oversights during development occurs in data conversion or migration. New DDP applications often require data from existing files. During DDP implementation, production data must be migrated or converted from the old system(s). In performing this task, data that will be confidential once the system is operational is often unthinkingly exposed. For example, temporary work files are created and used for a period ranging from a few hours to many weeks. Lists containing confidential data are often printed so that the functional user and DDP analyst can review them for accuracy. The conversion data files are rarely protected in any manner. After implementation, the disposal of these files and the printed work reports is often overlooked.

Systems documentation is not often included in confidentiality considerations. To ensure confidentiality, two measures should be taken. First, access to systems documentation must be secured in order to inhibit intelligent penetration. An understanding of the internals of the system is necessary for intelligent penetration, and systems documentation provides that understanding. Second, violations caused by inadvertent errors should be eliminated or minimized by imposing adequate controls on access to systems documentation and on modifications. By properly monitoring modifications, confidentiality problems can be identified before implementation.

Post-Implementation Oversights

Once a DDP system is implemented, there are even more potential confidentiality oversights. The following discussion is not exhaustive but is intended to give the reader a starting point for further considerations.

System Recovery Procedures. Confidentiality may be jeopardized during recovery after system failures. Because of the urgency of making the system available, normal procedures often are not followed. This usually occurs because controls for such circumstances were not previously thought out. The challenge for the DDP developer is to provide well-organized recovery procedures that ensure confidentiality without greatly extending recovery time. If well designed, controls can actually shorten recovery time by making the procedures more organized. Recovery training and actual dry runs should be used when feasible. Because of employee turnover and system changes, these dry runs should be repeated periodically.

Disaster Recovery. The same exposures and suggested protections also apply to disaster recovery. The physical distribution of both hardware and data in DDP systems inherently minimizes the effects of disasters. It does not, however, eliminate the need for well-thought-out recovery procedures. Clear assignment of responsibilities and disaster recovery training are necessary for security.

For both system and disaster recovery procedures, actual dry runs may not be feasible because of time, costs, or disruption of normal business. Alternatives to dry runs include simulation using a test system and role playing during paper walk-throughs. Planners should also consider the reasons against employing these techniques. Again, analysis of the confidentiality needs of the organization should determine the appropriate effort.

Program Modifications. A DDP environment has dispersed programs. These programs are often written by a central DDP development staff, particularly if the programs have confidentiality requirements. After installation, such programs must be secured against modification. As discussed earlier, these programs can be protected with passwords; however, intelligent penetration can occur if the password protection is circumvented. Auditing is the suggested means of locating breaches once the system is operational.

An additional or alternative precaution is to develop procedures that redisperse these programs from the central site by overlaying object code (executable program code). The object code should be redistributed at random intervals. When this is done, any unauthorized modifications made at remote sites are destroyed. Moving copies of the object code is more economical than recompiling programs and will minimize errors.

Courier Transport. Once DDP applications are operational, there are often times when data must be transported by courier rather than by a telecommunications network. The courier service for transporting confidential data should be reputable and bonded. In some cases a contract assigning liability should be negotiated. Containers for transporting data should be secured with locks and/or seals. Check-out and check-in times should be recorded, and normal elapsed times should be established in order to monitor delivery. In cases of stringent security needs, having more than one person accompany the data minimizes risk because criminal action then requires collusion.

Maintenance Personnel. Another frequent oversight is a lack of control over hardware maintenance personnel. Frequently these are vendor employees, and their access to the DDP environment is often not adequately examined. In some organizations, anyone with a toolbox and an attitude of confidence can gain access to the computer. How many organizations maintain a list of authorized personnel from a given vendor? Is there a procedure for keeping the list current as vendor personnel change? Are vendor personnel observed during the performance of their tasks? Are the visits logged, listing time and purpose?

Systems Review. In the DDP development cycle, a systems review should be conducted from six to nine months after initial installation. Initiating the review is the responsibility of the security officer. The major participants are the functional users and the auditing staff. The procedures used at implementation should be reviewed, and the following points should be considered:
- Are these procedures actually being practiced?
- Are they adequate?
- Are they too restrictive?
- Are they within established cost estimates?

The answers to such questions may lead to decisions that require additional management directives, training, procedural or system changes, and so on. The review will also improve communications and provide useful insights for future DDP development.

CONCLUSION

The success of DDP confidentiality measures begins with the understanding and commitment of all levels of management and the support of the entire organization. A case-by-case business analysis must be conducted. Cost analysis may be appropriate; in some instances, the nature of the organization may require confidentiality measures regardless of cost. In either case, quantification is difficult, and final decisions should be made at the management level rather than by the DDP analyst. This requires management awareness and good communication between functional management and the DDP developers. The security officer is an important link in this communication. As can be seen in the checklist in the Appendix, the developers, the users, the security officer(s), and the auditing department must cooperate in order to provide adequate protection for the organization's data resources.

APPENDIX

Checklist for Confidentiality in Distributed Systems

Task	Individual Responsible	Major Participants
1. Develop initial work plan.	PL	PA, U
2. Determine what data is to be protected.	U	SO, PL
3. Analyze business requirements.	U	PL
4. Preliminary system design	PL	PA
5. Preliminary controls	SO	U, PL
6. Revise work plan.	PL	PA, U, SO
7. Initial DDP system review	PL	U, SO, A, PA
8. Distribute review minutes.	PL	
9. Follow up on review items.	As assigned	PL
10. Develop details of implementation alternatives.	PL	PA, SO, U
11. Second DDP system review	PL	U, SO, A, PA
12. Distribute review minutes.	PL	
13. Follow up on review items.	As assigned	PL
14. Select hardware and/or software.	PL	U, SO
15. DDP system construction	PL	PA
16. Develop migration plan.	PL	U, SO, PA
17. Develop migration controls.	SO	U, PL
18. Develop testing controls.	PL	SO
19. Develop recovery plans.	SO	U, PL
20. Develop disaster plan.	SO	U, PL
21. Develop education plan.	U	PL, SO
22. Create user passwords, profiles, and/or encryption keys.	SO	U
23. Develop post-implementation audit plans.	SO	U, A
24. Develop post-implementation operational controls.	SO	U
25. Final DDP system review	PL	U, SO, A, PA
26. Education	U	PL, SO
27. Post-implementation audits	A	U, SO

Notes:
U   User
PL   DDP Project Leader
PA   DDP Programmer/Analyst
SO   Security Officer
A   Auditor

11 Operational Costs in Distributed Systems

by Raymond P. Wenig

INTRODUCTION

Each node in a distributed system is essentially a complete local data center that requires the same care and feeding (at reduced levels) needed for a central data center. In addition, a distributed system incurs costs for interconnection between nodes, equipment service, and technical and managerial support. Distributed systems also involve many hidden expenses (e.g., the cost of storage cabinets for data files at each location, the cost of carrying a sufficient inventory of all output forms at each location). These costs often add up to a sizable amount when assessed over the entire distributed system.

This chapter discusses the operational costs of a distributed system. It is assumed that the fixed investments in equipment, software, and technical training have already been evaluated, justified, and made. Operational costs include any cost incurred in the actual use of the system or in supporting the continued availability and enhancement of the distributed network. Controlling operational costs involves two major steps: a thorough evaluation of all cost items, and the implementation of practical procedures to minimize costs without incurring undue risks.

COST AREAS

The operational costs of a distributed system can be classified as follows:
- Local support equipment—the elements needed to properly support an operational distributed node
- Local expendables—the items to be consumed at a distributed node
- Local operations—the effort of support personnel to operate, service, supervise, and control the activities of a distributed node
- Interconnect services—the service activities performed at each site in support of the distributed network
- Remote services—the work performed for a distributed node at a remote node or at the host site
- Technical support—the professional assistance provided to evaluate and improve the local use of a distributed node

Each area is further divided in a cost checklist (see Appendix) with appropriate details, units of measure, and cost ranges. All costs are defined on a per-node basis.

DISTRIBUTED COST CONTROLS

As can be seen from the cost checklist, the operational costs of a distributed system include the costs of maintaining a small data center at each distributed node and the costs of managing a dynamic data flow among them. To keep the operational costs of a distributed system from escalating, the cost controls in a distributed system must also be distributed. The following sections describe cost controls that can be implemented in distributed systems.

Control of Consumables

A distributed system requires various consumable supplies at the local nodes. If these supplies are acquired in small quantities on a local basis, the cost can be exorbitant. Control of consumables can be achieved by creating a central purchasing and dispensing unit. This unit could be part of a central data center administration facility that performs many administrative functions for the host data center. The staff of this unit would have a thorough knowledge of available vendors and would work under volume-discount contracts that could easily be extended to include the distributed nodes.

In addition to providing a cost savings, a centralized consumables control unit can perform remote inventory control processing and reordering for the individual nodes. Although these tasks may require regular telephone calls to a site coordinator from the central control group, they can ensure consistent supply levels and reduce the amount of local effort spent in maintaining proper stock levels of consumable items.

Software Controls

The software in a distributed system often exists in several versions in order to support the varying needs of the individual nodes. One of the major causes of high costs in a distributed system is allowing each node to develop and/or modify its own software. The cost of the resulting duplication of training and work can be very high, and problems with inconsistency, errors, and documentation can be considerably increased.

The use of a central software repository and a single trained staff of designers and programmers to support all nodes can be advantageous from both cost- and operational-control standpoints. Although most distributed nodes need only part-time software support, the sophistication of interconnected data flows makes it advisable to employ highly skilled support personnel. One disadvantage of employing a central software support group, however, is that the members are not present at the local site to work directly with users. This problem can be reduced by using the system's communications network to distribute software changes and to collect user requests for

OPERATIONAL COSTS   139

changes. In addition, central technical specialists can use the network to conduct interactive training and change-evaluation sessions with the users.

Equipment Maintenance Controls

Ongoing maintenance in a distributed system is another major cost area that can be controlled centrally. Although the effect of the faults and failures of distributed equipment is usually felt first at the distributed node, it is often better to work through an internal maintenance coordinator than to call in the local maintenance vendor facility. With central control, problems and vendor response can be logged and monitored, and the consistency of vendor service at all nodes can be measured. If problems develop with the maintenance source, the clout of a central maintenance control group will greatly exceed that of local-node personnel.

Many equipment maintenance vendors are also developing central dispatch centers with toll-free call-in systems. This trend makes it even more useful to have a central maintenance controller to deal with the central vendor unit.

The internal maintenance controller can also monitor equipment performance at all locations, spot recurring faults, and conduct negotiations for revision or renewal of maintenance contracts. This type of control unit can realize cost savings by alleviating local user frustration, improving service and vendor support, and reducing local administrative procedures.

User Procedures and Attitudes

A distributed system involves some local independence in the use of computing services. Each node can, within limits, develop individual interpretations, adaptations, and extensions of system procedures. Local-unit staffs must be aware, however, that they are part of a larger system and must ensure that modifications at the local level do not hamper the operation of the total system.

These factors make periodic interaction among representatives from all nodes necessary. This interaction can take several forms, including:
- Nodal newsletters
- User group meetings
- Staff visits to other nodes
- Combining some nodes into teams

Interaction among nodes should make it easier for local staffs to:
- Share ideas
- Air complaints
- Review problems
- Discuss desirable changes in the system
- Form a cohesive user front to effectively deal with the central systems support functions
- Understand and improve the overall performance of the system

Although interaction among nodes may result in additional costs, the benefits for the total distributed system almost always make the effort cost-effective.

Local User Procedures

Most of the daily operational costs of a distributed system are incurred at the local level. The processing activities, personnel interfaces, response outputs, service problems, and expendable consumption all occur primarily at the local node. The only effective way to control these costs is to ensure that easy-to-use procedures for local users are developed, explained, and enforced at all nodes. Some of these procedures can be built into the information system as operator prompts, dialogues, control messages, operational tests, and balance steps. Others must be supplied as local documentation, and the users must be trained in the documentation's use.

Local procedures should be monitored through regular reviews (preferably by a roving outside team) to ascertain whether the procedures are being followed and are having the intended effect on operations and costs.

Performance Reporting

Like most businesses, nodes in a distributed system often settle into a comfortable level of local operation that might not be the most productive or cost-effective level for the total system. One way to reduce the overall operational costs of a distributed system is to institute competitive evaluation standards and reports that compare the performance of all nodes. This comparison can be done by regularly reporting on such operational statistics as:
- Volume
- Transaction costs
- Errors
- Business activity
- Peak transaction rates

This data can be monitored through the distributed network or manually collected by a central coordinator. The computed comparison for each node should be equalized for node size, processing volumes, and related differences to make the performance analysis equitable. The main goal of performance reporting is to establish a spirit of competition among the nodes and keep node staffs aware of their cost/performance ratios.

CONCLUSION

Cost control in a distributed system can be facilitated through the centralization of the major common administrative support functions (expendables, software, and maintenance control) and the development of effective standardized local procedures for operating the distributed nodes. In addition, a program of regular reviews of actual costs and problems should be implemented to check the operational costs at local and central sites against expected levels and to seek areas where improvement is needed.

APPENDIX

Distributed Systems Cost Checklist

Area	Cost Item	Units	Cost Range/Unit	Typical Levels Minimum	Typical Levels Average
Local Support Equipment	Data Storage Units	Cabinets	$100–$1,500	$100—Media File	$800—Metal Storage Cabinet with Locks
	Minidecollator	Tabletop, Electrically Operated	$300–$2,500	$0—Hand Separation	$800—Single-Carbon Separator Unit
	Miniburster	Tabletop, Electrically Operated	$800–$3,500	$0—Hand Bursting	$1,200—Adjustable Burster
	CRT User Workstation	Specially Designed Work Desk	$200–$800	$0—Use Existing Desks	$400—Per Station
	Paper Supply Storage Shelving	Storage Shelves or Cabinets	$250–$500	$150—Use Existing Space	$300—Install Special Shelving/Cabinets in Fire-Safe Area
	Data Storage Safe	Each	$0–$5,000	Use Existing Safe, or Trust to Luck	$2,500—6-sq ft Data Safe
	Magnetic Media Carrier	Each	$5–$200	1 for Each Type of Medium	2–3 for Each Type of Medium
	Small Paper Shredder	Each	$150–$750	$0—Rip Paper by Hand, or Ignore Security Problems	$500—Lightweight Wastebasket Shredder
	Large Trash Container with Fire Control Cover	Each	$80–$200	$0—Use Available Standard Wastebasket	$150 Medium-Size Container with Cover
	CO_2 Fire Extinguisher	Each	$65–$250	$65—1 Hand-held	$300—3 at Various Potential Fire Locations
	Plastic Equipment Covers	Each	$15–$50	$20—Use Locally Available Plastic Tarps	$50—Fitted Covers
Local Expendables	Stock Paper for Output	Cartons of 1000 Pages	$10–$75	1-Month Supply, 1 Ply	3-Month Supply, Several Plies
	Special Forms for Output	Cartons of 1000 Pages	$40–$95	1-Month Supply, Each Form	2–3-Month Supply, Each Form

Area	Cost Item	Units	Cost Range/ Unit	Typical Levels	
				Minimum	Average
Local Expendables (cont)	Printer Ribbons	Each	$3–$25	1-Month Supply	3-Month Supply
	Disk Media	Each	$5–$1,000	3 Times the Number of Operational Files	6 Times the Number of Operational Files
	Magnetic Tape	Each	$10–$35	5 Times the Number of Operational Files	10 Times the Number of Operational Files
	Replacement Disk Media	Each	$5–$1,000	1–3 per Quarter-Year	5–10 per Quarter-Year
	Replacement Tape Media	Each	$10–$35	1 per Month	3 per Month
	Forms Binders	Each	$3–$10	1 Dozen	3 Dozen
	Documentation Notebooks	Each	$5–$15	6	20
	Report Mailers	Each	$3–$20	3-Month Supply	6-Month Supply
	Media Labels	Box of 1,000	$30–$60	6-Month Supply	1-Year Supply
Local Operations	Systems Operator Effort	Hours per Day	$10–$15 per Hour	2 Hours per Day	4 Hours per Day
	Data Library Control	Hours per Week	$10–$15 per Hour	3 Hours per Week	10 Hours per Week
	User Coordination	Hours per Week	$10–$15 per Hour	1 Hour per Week	5 Hours per Week
	Data Operator Training and Performance Evaluation	Hours per Month	$10–$15 per Hour	1 Hour per Month	12 Hours per Month
	Facilities Space Cost	Square Foot	$6.50–$14 per Square Foot per Year (includes Lights, Heat, and air conditioning)	80 Square Feet	300 Square Feet for All Used Space
	Systems Power	Kilowatt Hours	$0.35–$0.60 per Kilowatt Hour	100 Kilowatt Hours	3,000 Kilowatt Hours
	Equipment Insurance	Per $1,000 of Protection	$3.50–$15	$25,000 of Protection	$80,000 of Protection
	Business Interruption Insurance	Blanket Value $100,000 Multi-Million	$300–$1,500 per $100,000	$0, Trust to Luck	$500,000 Major Catastrophe Coverage

OPERATIONAL COSTS 143

Area	Cost Item	Units	Cost Range/ Unit	Typical Levels	
				Minimum	Average
Local Operations (cont)	Equipment Maintenance	Monthly Fee for Parts/Labor Coverage	1.0–1.65 percent of the Total Equipment Cost	$150	$350
	Vendor Meetings and Reviews	Hours	Free–$25 per Hour	2 Hours per Quarter	1 Hour per Month
	Security Reviews	Hours	$25–$50 per Hour	2 Hours per Year	12 Hours per Year
	Purging Library Data Files	Hours	$15–$25 per Hour	2 Hours per Quarter	8 Hours per Quarter
Interconnect Services	Modems and Communications-Line Interfaces	Each	$25–$80 per Month Rental or $150–$450 Purchase	$150, Acoustic Coupler	$60 per Month, Telephone Company Data Set
	Communications Time	Varies with Service Selected	$5 per Call to $15 per Mile per Month	$100 per Month	$500 per Month
	Network Monitoring	Hours per Month	$35–$100 per Hour, including Equipment	$50 per Month	$200 per Month
	Retransmission of Errors	Minutes per Month	$2 per Call to $3 per Minute	$25 per Month	$50 per Month
Remote Services	Central/Host Computer Time	CPU Minutes	20–200 Minutes per Month at Variable Rates	20 Minutes	60 Minutes
	Remote Audit Testing of Local Data	Minutes per Month	10–60 Minutes per Month at an Average Cost of $5 per Minute	$0, Depend on Good Luck	$100–20 Minutes
	Review Complaints from Nodes	Minutes per Month	30–60 Minutes per Month at $25 per Hour	$10	$25
	Plan/Build Nodal Enhancements	Hours per Month	2–20 Hours per Month at $25 per Hour	$50	$200
Technical Support	Program Enhancements	Hours	$20–$30 per Hour	$100 per Month	$300 per Month
	Problem Reviews	Hours	$20–$30 per Hour	$20 per Month	$100 per Month
	Long-Range Planning	Hours	$30–$50 per Hour	$100 per Quarter	$500 per Quarter
	Technical Training	Hours	$25–$40 per Hour	$25 per Month	$100 per Month

12 The Relationship between Distributed Processing and Office Automation

by Joseph G. Robertson

INTRODUCTION

Today's typical office worker has become very skillful in performing a variety of information processing tasks and then using the information to make decisions and take actions. The information explosion, in fact, has caused the amount of information crossing an average worker's desk to more than double every six years. Office managers are faced with a situation in which there is more information to process, store, and find; unfortunately, there hasn't been a concomitant increase in the number of people to perform these functions. One indication of the severity of this paper blizzard is that the typical office worker now has four filing cabinets of information; projections indicate that there will be eight such cabinets per worker in the next five years. What is especially alarming about this vast amount of stored information is that 85 percent of it will never be looked at again.

Reducing the amount of physical storage and automating many of the repetitive labor-intensive tasks associated with the information explosion, as well as those requiring calculations, recordkeeping, and information retrieval, have become major goals of business management. The objective of automating these functions is to improve the generation, distribution, processing, presentation, storage, and retrieval of information in a cost-effective manner, thus increasing the overall productivity of the office worker. Computing technology is a major means of achieving these objectives.

Three major computer-oriented approaches for improving office productivity are currently available: DDP, small business computers, and WP systems. The use of all of these computer-oriented approaches will continue, and their capabilities will be expanded. The functions of these three types of systems, however, will merge, and an integrated information and information processing environment will evolve. DDP will become the predominant means of providing computer support to users. In addition, distributed office information systems will parallel and overlap the development of DDP systems. This chapter discusses the current relationship between DDP systems and office information systems and examines the possibilities for integration.

BACKGROUND

Computing support for office functions is not new—it has been used for more than three decades. What is new is the manner in which DP support is delivered to the office, as is the trend toward an integrated information environment.

Batch Mode. The earliest use of DP was in the batch production mode. In the eyes of many users, the seeming objective of batch processing is to produce miles of computer-generated reports on orders, inventories, personnel, sales, budgets, and other financially oriented information. This paper blizzard taxed the ingenuity of the functional professionals who now had to develop effective means of sorting and using more information than they ever had before. It also established the "data processing factory" as an organization separate and apart from the organizations using the data.

Online Access. As computing and communications technology evolved, CRT terminals were introduced, and online access to vast computer data bases became an alternative to computer printouts. Some of the earliest applications involved airline reservation systems, order entry, inventory control and warehouse management, and resource management and allocation. Nontechnical office workers could establish, query, and update critical business information, and all necessary personnel could access the same central data base. Users began to take a more active role in the use and control of the computing resources.

Minis and Micros. The introduction of the high-performance, low-cost minicomputer in the early 1970s prompted the development of even more online systems. Initially these systems tended to be local in nature and dedicated to specific functional applications. Since local data could not be easily shared or merged with data from other systems, however, discrete, limited applications began to proliferate. This turn of events was viewed as an operational threat and cost liability to the centralized computing philosophy of that period. During this same time, the use of microprocessor systems dedicated to WP became more prevalent in offices.

The Evolution of DDP. By the mid-1970s, companies had begun to capitalize on the advantages of minicomputers for DP; many of the initial limitations of minicomputer use were overcome through the evolution of the DDP concept. With the distributed approach, information is stored and processed at the location where these functions can be accomplished most cost-effectively. DDP also allows users with the smallest system to access the capabilities of the largest host computers.

Key Elements of DDP in the Office

Although the concept of distributed processing is somewhat broad, most DDP systems are composed of the following basic elements:

- Local intelligent devices (e.g., workstations, WP systems, or minicomputer systems) provide local support for specific functions and are connected to other intelligent devices or systems through a communications network for augmented processing and/or storage capabilities.
- One of the intelligent nodes in the network can serve as a host, exercising direct control over the network. In addition, networks can be established in a hierarchical fashion, or all nodes in the network can operate with each other in a peer relationship.
- Functions, data, and processing are distributed among the intelligent elements in the network, with the actual assignments being made on the basis of cost/performance trade-offs.
- The major functions performed by these distributed office information systems include:
  —Word/text processing
  —Office information storage, retrieval, and management
  —Office DP
  —Office information distribution
  —Remote data and job entry to other nodes or to the host
- Generally, local office systems will perform office information management functions but will only initiate DP functions to be executed on other systems.

Keys to Success. The keys to the success of this integrated information environment are standardization and compatibility. The same terminal that performs WP must support electronic mail and must interface with the DP services of the host computer. Local data bases must be compatible with each other and with data stored on host computers so that convenient information exchange can occur. Most important, the systems must be compatible with the needs and capabilities of the people who will use them in the office environment.

In summary, the technology for delivering computing support to the office is available. In addition, there is a considerable body of experience in making the technology accessible to professional and clerical personnel in performing highly specialized functions. Supporting the highly generalized activities of the typical office secretary and general office worker, however, is a more difficult undertaking. The remainder of this chapter will address what is required and what must be done to bring about the desired results.

APPLICATIONS

In order to define the relationship between DDP and office automation, let us consider the five specific areas in which office automation may be applicable:
- Information generation (including word, text, and graphics)
- Information storage, retrieval, and management
- Information processing (including data entry and application programming)

- Information presentation
- Information distribution

Information Generation

Creating office letters and reports is a personal activity involving the interaction of the originator and his or her clerical support. Conventional small WP systems at the local level offer a cost-effective way of supporting these small-volume, relatively simple, short-lived products. Activities involving greater complexity, larger volumes, and longer product life, however, generally necessitate the use of the resources of larger computers (i.e., distributed systems or a host computer). For example, the integration of graphics information into textual documents, the creation of a complex document by many people at different locations, and the logical extraction of information from a complex data base for inclusion in a document probably exceed the capability of a conventional WP system.

Two-Tier Capability. To perform these complex activities requires a two-tier WP capability operating on the same terminal but not necessarily on the same computing device. User-friendly operating procedures could be employed to create, edit, store, and distribute simple documents. As more complex materials are created and more storage capacity demanded, additional system functions and procedures could be invoked; these functions and procedures would utilize the resources of a local distributed system or the host. The place where processing occurs or information is stored is the system's responsibility and would not concern operators.

This augmented capability can reduce a significant amount of the labor-intensive portion of document generation. Using a financial data base, for example, the user can create financial tables that are checked automatically and then converted into a graphic representation for direct incorporation into a document. Digital scanners can convert existing graphics information into processable form that can also be directly incorporated. These capabilities eliminate the hours of work generally associated with hand calculation, table layout, graphics artwork, cutting, pasting, and document editing.

Improving Data Input. Another aspect of information generation that can benefit from augmented capabilities is the data input function. The office terminal can be used to complete standard office forms (e.g., travel expense forms) and can also serve as a data entry terminal for updating computer files. When coupled with digitized voice storage, the same storage medium can be used as a centralized dictation tank, further improving the productivity of those involved in information generation.

Information Storage, Retrieval, and Management

Distributed office systems may have the greatest applicability in storing, retrieving, and managing information. Large-volume, low-cost digital information storage and retrieval is becoming a reality, given the current state of development of peripheral devices. As more information is created electronically, and as it becomes more economical to convert hard-copy information to electronic form through OCR and digital scanners, centralized electronic files will become more significant. In the future, when office information is created, it will be immediately available for automatic distribution and electronic archiving. Such an arrangement eliminates the need to retain multiple copies of a single document under different filing categories. In addition, recipients of a document will not have to keep their own copies of it. This does not mean that hard-copy files will disappear; they will continue to be used for frequently accessed reference files and for documents with a high percentage of graphics material (including approval signatures).

Hierarchical Storage. For that portion of office information that is stored electronically, a hierarchical storage scheme will be used. Active local work files and correspondence will be retained on the local office system while they are in frequent use. As use becomes less frequent, the information may be destroyed, or it may be transferred to a host system's mass storage device. Eventually the information will be moved to offline storage media for permanent archiving. In all cases, however, the information (unless destroyed) will be cataloged and will be retrievable through various logical search arguments.

Information Processing

Information processing in the office environment can take several forms and can occur at many locations. In its simplest form, basic DP functions (e.g., sorting and simple arithmetic operations) can be directly associated with the local WP capability. At the next level, information can be cataloged for retrieval using Boolean or keyword search arguments. Information can be retrieved from the local files of a distributed system or from a central data bank.

Advanced Applications. More complex functions involving data entry and edit (supporting such activities as order entry or resource management) could significantly aid many office workers. Again, the data base could be decentralized, distributed, or centralized. Using corporate data bases and the resources of the host computer in conjunction with a distributed processing system, administrators and managers could use such advanced applications as financial data planning, analysis, and modeling. Finally, the office terminal could serve as a programming terminal to gain full use of the DP and storage resources of the host computer.

Information Presentation

Presentation of office information also can take various forms. In moving toward a paperless society, soft copy (or information displayed on a screen) will become increasingly important. Reviewing correspondence and retrieving information will be accomplished without ever going to hard copy. Generally, information that lends itself to soft-copy presentation will be moved among computing systems: the requesters or recipients of such information need not know (nor concern themselves with) the actual storage location of the information.

Hard-copy information will also be available in many forms and from diverse devices. Local office printers will provide convenient, high-quality, medium-volume output of both textual and graphics information; such printers will support the output of DP, WP, and electronic mail services. Very high-speed, high-quality printers will be used with distributed office systems for supporting host-computer text editing output, large-size document transfer, and batch electronic mail.

Microform input and output in distributed office systems will provide greater flexibility for the exchange and local storage of hard-copy information. Centralized microform storage also will be available; digital scanning and information compression will allow for the rapid transmission and reconstruction of images on remote terminals.

Information Distribution

One of the most significant aspects of office automation will be electronic information distribution. With automated equipment installed in a company's offices, rapid, low-cost worldwide communication will become a reality. Communications networks and network services will move computer data; office information; electronic mail; and digitized voice, video, and facsimile among these locations. Announcements and items of general interest will be distributed to all locations simultaneously through broadcast mail, with all authorized personnel accessing a single electronic copy at each location.

INTEGRATING THE APPLICATIONS

To help the reader better understand the integration of these applications, this section discusses a typical technical and operational environment that is capable of supporting diverse applications in a distributed processing network. The organization described is a large, multilocation company (the same concept can be scaled down for smaller organizations).

The XYZ Manufacturing Corporation

The XYZ Manufacturing Corporation is a $500 million manufacturer and distributor of automotive components. Basic DP capability is provided to various company locations by three large regional computing centers located in the East, Midwest, and West. Each center has one or more large-scale computers with massive storage and processing capabilities. The centers are connected by high-volume satellite and terrestrial communications links that provide rapid information exchange. These links also allow the company's total information processing load to be shared among the different centers.

Time-zone differences in the various plant locations result in different peak-load times; this fact makes dynamic load balancing a cost-effective means of utilizing the computing resources of the company.

Local Systems. Within each geographic region are dozens of sales offices and plant locations that depend on the regional computers for large-volume information storage and retrieval and DP. All plants and most of the offices have their own smaller computers with local terminals for supporting some of their data and office information processing and storage requirements. The remaining offices only have terminals with which to access the resources of the regional host computer.

Specific configurations, capabilities, and features of the local computer systems vary, although they conform to company-wide technical and operational standards. As a result, all terminals can gain access to the corporate data communications network to take advantage of the DP and storage resources of any of the regional computing centers. The terminals can also communicate information to any other computer or terminal in the network.

Specific Applications. Local systems support such specific office applications as WP and information management. Some of the smaller offices have dedicated WP systems in addition to terminals for accessing the host. A few are totally dependent on the host for all data and office information processing support.

The XYZ Manufacturing Corporation is clearly employing DDP, sharing computing resources and data for their DP activities. The office information processing, however, tends to be more decentralized, with the central computing and communications network supporting electronic information distribution and archiving of selected office information.

This computing and telecommunications environment can meet the processing and storage requirements of each location, while making available the full power of host computing and data storage. This environment is effective because:
- Most terminals are multifunction (WP and DP) and have access to both distributed systems and host systems.
- An integrated computing/communications network has been established.
- Technical and operating standards have been established.
- Data is processed and information stored on the device and at the location where it can be done most cost-effectively.

TECHNOLOGY

Distributed processing in the office environment depends on two basic areas of technology: computing and telecommunications. These are augmented by extensive human engineering and systems integration. Significant advances have been made in computing and communications technology;

during the past five years, the industry has gained considerable experience in designing and implementing distributed processing systems. In marked contrast, a great deal is yet to be learned about developing distributed office information systems. Research continues on effective man/machine interfaces for the complex psychological, sociological, and decision-oriented office environment.

Distributed Data Processing

As the name suggests, distributed data processing involves the distribution of DP and storage functions among two or more intelligent devices. A device can be as simple as an intelligent terminal or as complex as a large host computer. In most cases, these devices are separated geographically but are connected by telecommunications links. A distributed function can be as simple as data entry from a remote terminal to a host computer—only data editing occurs at the intelligent terminal. In contrast, a distributed function can occur almost totally in a remote system, with only complex calculations or summary sorting occurring in the host.

Networking Alternatives. Some distributed systems involve a communications network with a host at the hub and a number of distributed elements individually connected to it by radials (a star network). Others are structured hierarchically, with many smaller systems connecting to a few mid-sized systems that are, in turn, connected to a single host computer. In peer-related systems all computers are equal and somewhat independent, although communications and information exchange can take place. The choice of network architectures is a function of the computing philosophy of the company; ideally, the company's computing philosophy is derived from its organizational structure and the applications that are distributed. The technology to support any of these network architectures is currently available.

Design Trade-Offs. Problems arise in developing DDP systems when planners and designers feel compelled to select from among a number of polarized alternatives. Distributed processing lies somewhere between decentralized and centralized systems. Planners, therefore, should identify their organization's computing philosophy and then determine what and how much processing should be distributed and what and how much data should be centralized or made redundant for each specific application.

Similar trade-offs should be made in the areas of cost versus performance, telecommunications versus computing costs, centralized versus decentralized responsibility and authority, manual versus automated functions, and risk versus opportunity. There are, of course, no simple rules for making these decisions: each decision has an interactive effect on the others, and each corporate environment is different.

The Advantages of DDP. Companies that have addressed and resolved the major distributed processing issues are probably in a better position to

DDP AND OFFICE AUTOMATION   153

exploit distributed office information systems than are those companies with a predominantly centralized or decentralized computing philosophy. The companies that have adopted DDP have the advantage of an in-place computing/communications network, existing technical and operational standards and procedures, the organizational structure for centrally controlling a complex technical environment, and an awareness of both the opportunities and disadvantages of distributing processing and data.

Distributed Office Information Systems

Distributed office information systems can come in all of the varieties and architectures that are characteristic of DDP systems. In configuring such systems for the office, the functions to be performed must be specified, and the relationship of these functions to other office systems and DP systems in the network must be established. For example, if the primary function is local WP, then the relation to the host might be for electronic document distribution or archival storage or for access to such peripherals as laser printers, photocomposition, or computer output microform. If the primary function of an office system is local financial management, however, there may be no relation to other systems and only a data reporting relationship with the host.

Clearly identifying the intended functions of an office system makes it possible to determine the magnitude of local processing power, data storage, specialized peripherals, and the communications required to support the functions.

Multifunction Office Systems. In the integrated environment of the future, office systems will be expected to serve many functions, including WP, local information management, remote data entry and access, and remote job entry to a host computer. To perform these functions effectively, an office information system should probably be established as a node in a DDP environment, with its attendant networking concepts, technical standards, and operating procedures.

One of the reasons WP systems have multiplied is that relatively complex editing and data manipulation functions can be performed in a fairly simple manner by nontechnical personnel. In developing distributed office systems, this concept of simple operation must be continued because users will be professional, management, and clerical personnel rather than computer experts and programmers.

EQUIPMENT SELECTION

Currently, many minicomputer and microprocessor systems have the technical capability to support DDP and/or distributed office information systems. Specifically, they have the capability to communicate data and textual information in a compatible fashion.

Some vendors have developed operating systems that are particularly well suited to DDP and that simplify the process of implementing data bases and application software for the distributed processing environment. Other vendors have developed user-friendly software for word processing and information access and are beginning to address the integrated information environment for office applications. Still others have stressed the development of application software for such areas as financial DP, payroll/personnel, and order entry/inventory control. Vendors, however, have not yet integrated all of these capabilities and offered them as a single system. Integrated and distributed office information systems are currently developed by users, not purchased from vendors (integrating these capabilities requires a significant development investment).

Selection Issues

Four major issues must be addressed when selecting equipment:
- What is the primary intended use of the system today: office automation or DDP?
- What growth in capacity and functional capability is anticipated over the life of the equipment?
- What capabilities are currently available on the candidate systems?
- What development efforts are required of the company and the vendor, and what assistance will the vendor provide?

If the primary near-term use of the system is to support DDP functions with little or no need for WP, a variety of candidate systems are available. Some of these systems also have WP software available, enabling future expansion into this functional area. If the primary intended use of the system is for office automation—particularly WP with an interface to such peripherals as optical character readers and photocomposition devices—then the selection is narrowed to those vendors specializing in the WP approach to office automation. Generally, sufficient communications capability is available on these systems to allow asynchronous and bisynchronous communications to other word processors and a host computer. A few of the newer WP systems operate in a shared operating system environment, allowing both WP and DP to occur on the same office workstation. The development of local application software and access to the resources of the host computer provide considerable growth potential and functional capabilities.

Other factors that must weigh heavily in the selection of equipment include:
- Security provisions—Because office information can be crucial to the operation of the company, it must be protected from accidental or intentional access, destruction, and change. This is currently an area of major weakness in both DDP and office information systems.
- System availability—Vital information will be stored and processed on these systems. System reliability and vendor responsiveness in providing maintenance are the two key factors in ensuring that this information will be available on a timely basis.
- System growth and upgrade potential—If the selected system is to have a reasonably useful life, it should have considerable growth potential in

main memory, disk storage capacity, and in the number and variety of peripherals it can support.

Identifying Leading-Edge Vendors. When selecting equipment, it is important to remember that while all the capabilities of the integrated and distributed office information system are not yet available, the forward-looking vendors are working toward this objective. Reviewing their product development histories and carefully evaluating their current products will help to identify leading-edge vendors.

CONCLUSION

DDP is proving to be a cost-effective means of providing computing resources and services to users in larger companies. The primary benefits of DDP have been responsiveness to online DP requirements, greater user involvement and responsibility for the system, and satisfactory cost/performance trade-offs. Office automation in the form of WP, small business systems, and personal computing is also leading to increases in productivity.

In the future, the capabilities that are now supported by independent systems will be integrated and supported by a more comprehensive distributed processing environment. This will come about as vendors develop more sophisticated products and as more companies implement their own integrated information environment and distributed office information system.